THE PROPHECY OF
SOLOMON

MIKE BATES

www.mwbates.com

ISBN 978-1-64515-083-1 (paperback)
ISBN 978-1-64515-084-8 (digital)

Christian Faith Publishing, Inc.
832 Park Avenue
Meadville, PA 16335
www.christianfaithpublishing.com

Cover Design, designed by: **Hanni Plato**

Printed in the United States of America

Through scripture God has hidden and revealed the mysteries of His Kingdom and plans. Beneath the surface of the Song of Solomon lies a hidden treasure of the mystery and revelation of the Church. Concealed and revealed in the Song are such things as: the first and second coming of Jesus, the crucifixion, the arrival of the Holy Spirit, and the Marriage Supper of the Lamb.

The Prophecy of Solomon examines the Song of Solomon as prophetic look into the Church Age, revealing both the individual and corporate Bride's journey of discovery, first of the King, Jesus, and then herself as a Bride and "Church" becoming. In Revelation 19:7 we read: "the Bride has made herself ready." If the Church is to be made ready she must know her responsibilities as a betrothed Bride, and she must understand who and what she is to become.

Presented with and accepting the King's offer of betrothal, this once broken, hopeless, enslaved individual is given a new name, a new identity, authority, and a new occupation. See how the Holy Spirit inspired Solomon to portray her journey of transformation through salvation, sanctification, growth, awakening, and healing that enables her to become a glorious, evangelizing, reflection of her Bridegroom King, Jesus.

CONTENTS

INTRODUCTION

Chuck Missler once said: "The 66 books which we call the Bible consti-tute a highly integrated message system…every word, every place name, every detail was apparently placed there (in the original) deliberately as part of an overall intricate plan."[1]

With any exegesis of the *Song of Solomon* there is a temptation to dissect every word or line. Another challenge is how to begin; perhaps best is a brief statement regarding Rabbinic Jewish Hermeneutics. In simple terms, scripture can be studied and interpreted on four primary levels, the simple literal meaning, the deeper symbolic and allegorical meaning, the parabolic or comparative meaning, and the secret hidden and revelatory information within the text[2] *From Pardes.* This will be an examination from the perspective of the deeper symbolic meaning and the secret hidden meaning within the text. Exploring at times the metaphor within the lines and digging deep into the etymology and meanings within the Hebraic words, we will discover how the Holy Spirit moved upon Solomon, with or without his knowledge, to describe the Bridegroom Jesus, to describe the Bride, Jesus's Church, and the Dispensation of Grace we refer to as the Church Age. We will piece together what we know empirically from scripture to show the prophetic nature of the Song of Solomon and derive from what we should by now know from other prophetic passages what the Bride can anticipate in the near future.

Having said this, I am one who believes the Bible to be the iner-rant Word of God, inspired by the Holy Spirit, written by Hebrew men, with the exception of Luke, from the Hebraic culture and view-point. I believe the literal interpretation of scripture while also rec-ognizing the Bible incorporates symbolism, metaphor, poetry, and parable which in Old and New Covenant alike, *Hosea 12:10* and *Matthew 13* pointing out, the Lord uses in order to teach, conceal, and reveal the mysteries of the Kingdom of God. So beyond the literal meaning there are instances, in particular in parable and poetry where we can, with caution, look at possible or probable deeper meaning, at what could be understood, and what the Hebrew words conceivably illustrate or represent.

And if we are to grasp the revelation and hidden mysteries the Holy Spirit is attempting to convey, all of which including historical accounts must be examined from a dynamic not merely a static point of view. In other words all scripture, even the historical records and the manner in which the Holy Spirit communicated them are, as the word of God is, living and active *(Hebrews 4:12)*. Within scriptural accounts, poems, and parables are not only records of the past but at times, foretelling's of the future, Solomon giving indication of this truth in *Ecclesiastes 1:9 and 3:15*. The most easily understood of this concept is seen in the account of Ruth and Boaz, which we know is both historical and a prophetic revelation of the Messiah and His Church, in particular the inclusion of Gentiles in His Church.

While the Song of Solomon has tremendous value in its literal and historical interpretation, I believe from a prophetic viewpoint it stands next to the Book of Ruth as one of the most profound anticipations of the Church. Song of Solomon is far more than a depiction of the intimate relationship between a man and woman, as has been understood for centuries, it portrays God's love for His Bride Israel and Jesus's relationship with His Bride, The Church, in the past, the present, and the future *(see Isa. 54:5; Jer. 2:2; Ezek. 16:8–14; Hos. 2:16–20; 2 Cor. 11:2; Eph. 5:23–25; Rev. 19:7–9, 21:9)*.

This exegesis of the Song of Solomon is not intended to be comprehensive, it is to examine portions of the mystery "secret" of the Church both concealed and prophetically revealed in the Song. Many scriptures prophesied and pointed as shadows to the Messiah in order to give us a mental picture, to give us knowledge of Christ, but Song of Solomon is different. The purpose of Song of Solomon is to take us beyond an intellectual level of knowledge; its purpose is not only to teach us, but also to reach our heart and soul, to touch our emotions, feelings, and to ignite our passion for Christ.

Man of course is limited and constrained by time but God is not, He like His word given to Man is from outside the boundaries of our linear time. Scriptures tells us that God declares the end from the beginning, meaning in simplest terms He knows and has revealed through His Word history in advance. I believe Song of Solomon is just such a message, one from Jewish King, Jesus, to His Bride, the Church, of the marriage and wedding, the New Testament as well bearing out, that will take place in the tradition of the time and culture in which the King came to His garden and vineyard to seek and purchase that Bride.

Having said that and before attempting to interpret this song prophetically one more basic foundational cornerstone upon which we build is required; as it is the portrait of the love story and marriage of a Jewish King and his Bride it necessitates we who are Gentiles possess at minimum a basic understanding of the ancient Jewish wedding process. A process referred to repeatedly by Jesus concerning Himself and His Church many may never have noticed.

To keep it simple and limited for this discussion I will break down the ancient Jewish wedding and marriage process into six stages.

1.   Betrothal: *Kiddashin (kid·du·shin)*

The first step was the Betrothal initiated by the Bridegroom or His father, which in the ancient Hebrew culture rendered the Couple legally Husband and Wife in what we would consider a limited sense (no co-habitation). Remember Jesus sent by the Father initiated our Relationship!

Betrothal required the payment of The Bride Price. This payment constituted something of value given as gifts for the Bride and was the guarantee or promise of the future union. This payment legally insured the marital relationship between the Man and Woman.

The Price, as we know Jesus paid was Himself, His Crucifixion and death on The Cross.

Acceptance by the Bride of the gifts and the drinking of a first cup of wine referred to as the *Cup of Sanctification* completed rite of Betrothal known in Hebrew as kiddashin (kid·du·shin), meaning "sanctification" (purified, made holy, set apart/separated or dedicated unto). The next stage in the marriage process reveals something I think many Christians fail realize concerning the importance and timing of the sacrament of baptism. After the completed rite of *kiddashin* and prior to the wedding the Bride was required to undergo a ceremonial rite of purification by the immersion in living water, the Mikvah. The Mikvah baptism indicated a separation from a former way to a new way. In the case of marriage, it indicates leaving an old life for a new life with your spouse *(Genesis 2:23–24, Ephesians 5:31)*. In Jewish tradition and culture the bride undergoing this ceremonial washing among other things represented a change of authority. She, as it were, comes out from under her father's, or brother's authority to come under her husband's authority. And, as immersing oneself in the mikvah is considered a spiritual rebirth, she is as a result severed from her past.

2.   The return of the Bridegroom to His Father's house.

Following the betrothal ceremony was a time of separation, one in which the Bride prepared herself for a new life with her husband and one in which the Bridegroom went back to his father's house to prepare a home for his Bride. Before he would leave, he would make a statement to the bride of this nature "I go to prepare a place for you; if I go, I will return for you." This is the same statement Jesus made in *John 14:1–3*.

This is the period we are now in and have been for two thousand years and which we can see alluded to in Solomon's Song.

3.   Return of Bridegroom for His Bride

When the Father of the Bridegroom gave permission, the Bridegroom would return unannounced, often at Midnight, to the home of the Bride's father and take his wife thus being referred to as the Thief in the Night, *(1 Thessalonians 5:2)*. It should be noted that part of the Bride's preparation was to have a lamp ready with oil should He come for Her in the night!

Jesus uses this illustration as He refers to His coming in *Matthew 24–25.*

Nevertheless, at this point the Jewish Bride was said to be stolen or caught up "snatched away" as the bridegroom came with a shout *Matthew 25:6* and with the blowing of a shofar (trumpet) *(1 Thessalonians 4:16–17, Revelation 4:1)*.

4.   The Consummation *nisuin*: Bride and Bridegroom entering into the Wedding Chamber

The full marriage, known in Hebrew as *nesu'in* (from a word meaning "elevation"), is completed by the chupah (coming under the canopy). The bride is carried to *Chupah* (bridegroom's canopy, Heaven) in the *Appiryon*, the Bridal Carriage or The Brides Chariot, for the wedding ceremony at His Father's house where her groom, adorned with a garland of roses and myrrh awaited her.

The bride and groom would then go to the wedding chamber, or *chadar* in Hebrew, to consummate the marriage.

5.   The Wedding Supper at the Bridegroom's Father's House

Following the official marriage was the Bridal week of celebration; during this phase the consummation of the marriage would take place as well as the wedding supper *(Revelation 19:7—9)*. At this stage the couple will share a second cup of wine together, referred to as the Cup of Consummation *(Matthew 26:29)*.

6.   The Public appearance of the consummated Couple— *"The Return to Her Home"*

The journey through this prophetic song must be done from the perspective of the Hebraic roots of Christianity. Christ must also remove the veil from our eyes (*2 Corinthians 3:14--16)* if we are to see clearly the deeper message of Jesus, ourselves, and The Church as a body.

As we examine this poetic work, contemplating the deeper meaning of the symbolism interwoven throughout we find:

It speaks of Jesus's pursuit of and payment for His bride, His Church.

It reveals our recognition of our unrighteousness.

It speaks of our accepting His offer, making us righteous and clean.

It outlines our betrothal by accepting the price Jesus paid for our sanctification.

It describes Jesus adoration for His Church.

It is an expression of mutual and individual love.

It reveals the Bride's awakening.

It describes the sleeping Church.

It relates Jesus departure and the Church being caught up to Him.

It describes the marriage and consummation between Christ and His Church.

It reveals the Church's return to earth with Christ.

CHAPTER 1
The Principal Characters

Hindsight is twenty-twenty the old adage goes. Viewing Song of Solomon from this side of the Cross we recognize it as, and as most commentators agree, the story of Christ and His Bride, the Church. From the first line it is evident that this song is far more than one written of the love between a man and his bride. For if it were an ordinary love song it would not be titled the Song of Songs. No, it would be as Paul McCartney so famously put it, just another silly love song.

That it was penned nearly one thousand years before the first coming of Jesus; we can infer that the undercurrent running throughout the Song is prophetic. A prophecy that from its beginning depicts a Bride brought into covenant relationship and intimacy; one brought into and made to be a "sheep of His pasture." We read of an evangelizing Church, one to whom He speaks and whose voice she hears.

The principle characters in the Song are: the Bride who we now know is the Church, the Bridegroom, Jesus, and His Friends, the Daughters of Jerusalem, who more than the chorus refrain in our song represent the nation of Israel. Jesus we know, as prophesied in *Zechariah 13:6*, was wounded in the house of His friends. And perhaps at times in the Song we might view them as those who are outside covenant relationship with the Bridegroom. Also evident is the King to whom Solomon is referring is more than himself for he speaks of him as a shepherd. His father David was a shepherd as is

Jesus, the Son of David, yet Solomon the king would have certainly assigned this job to others *(Song 1:7–8, John 10:1–16)*.

A note to men: Men, we must not feel uncomfortable being likened to a Bride for the woman in Song of Solomon represents all believers, individual male and female. A symbol validated by Paul in *Romans 7:1–4*.

The Bride and the Mystery of the Bride

The first voice to speak is that of the Bride. As Paul plainly stated in *Ephesians 5:32* The Church, The Bride, is a hidden mystery in the Old Testament. In order to understand things hidden or concealed one must know or have the key principal unlocking those mysteries, secrets, and hidden things. The most basic principle then to be understood is that as a means of protecting and sealing a particular message, the Lord has concealed within various text a deeper meaning one beyond the surface level one He desires us to discover. To paraphrase Solomon in Proverbs 25:2: It is the glory of God to conceal a matter, it is the glory of man to search that matter out. Jesus Himself making it clear the principles and mysteries of the Kingdom of Heaven are both hidden and revealed in the parables.

Jewish scholars understood that the Torah contained an inner dimension. Jesus referred to this when He said to them "you search the Scriptures for in them you think you have eternal life and these are they which testify of Me" *(John 5:29; Luke 24:27; Hebrews 10:7; Psalm 40:7)*. They also knew that when the Messiah did come He would reveal the hidden mysteries of the word, see for example the story of the woman at the well in *John 4:25*. Jesus is the hidden mystery, who He is, what He did, does, and will do is as well concealed and revealed in the Scriptures. And as stated, His Bride is likewise veiled in the Scriptures as Paul writes in *Ephesians. 3:3–5, 9* and *Colossians 1:25–27*.

The term Bride in Song of Solomon, kallah (kal-law"), refers to a bride before marriage, one betrothed or promised, points to the Church awaiting the Marriage Supper. From the root word kalal (kaw-lal"), meaning to be complete, perfected, or made perfect she is as made to be as Paul proclaims in Colossians 2:10 of Jesus's Church complete in Him. And again, in Hebrews 10:14 the writer declares: Jesus has perfected, made perfect and complete, those being sanctified, those who have entered into intimate relationship with Him; or might we say those betrothed to Him.

The Bride we find is referred to as the Shulamite. What is in a name? Much when we speak of the Bible. Prophetic in itself is the name Shulamite, for in it we see who she is to become. Also important is to note the term Shulamite is an adjective not a noun; it is actually a description. So what we actually read in the Song of Solomon is a depiction of the Bride. In Hebrew adjectives follow nouns so I like to think of it this way: where we see the Bride described or defined as something it is that she has been made, or has become such after the fact, in other words she does not start out in such state, or status, she becomes. Everything about Jesus, His work of reconciliation, propitiation, redemption, and restoration is so that we can "become." To see who she is becoming we must first look at the King, Solomon, whose name means peaceful, Solomon is from the word shalom meaning peace, friend, great, good health, perfect, and happy. Shalom is from a root word shalam, which means to make amends, finish, make good, to be safe, recompense, restore. Shulamite, which is also derived from shalam, then indicates she has been amended, made peaceful, complete, finished, whole, safe, recompensed, restored. We see in the Song that as she betroths herself to this king, coming under and assuming the name of her bridegroom, with His name upon her, she is transformed from one state of being into another. Her story is of one transformed from rags to righteousness as she experiences a new birth, a starting over, a change in life, and status. She is a Bride becoming, one in the process of change and the portrait of grace and beauty; she is being made pleasing, attractive, suitable, and appropriate for the King.

Shulamite is also thought to be the equivalent of Shunammite signifying a woman from Shunem, a city in the inheritance of Issachar (he will bring a reward; recompense) where Elisha raised the woman's son from the dead. So what do we see symbolized in that the Bride in Song of Solomon is perhaps from the tribe of *Issachar*? First, Jacob prophesied in *Genesis 49:14–15* that Issachar would carry a burden and become a band of slaves. Second, Issachar is derived from two words: The first word *nasa* or *nasah (naw-saw')* meaning to lift, carries a number of literal and figurative meanings such as pardon, raise up, receive, forgive, carry away, desire, obtain, marry; and the second word *sakar (saw-kawr')* meaning wages, hire, reward, worth, comes from a word meaning to purchase. Issachar then is figurative of the Church. The Church, once slaves to sin the reward of which is death, has been purchased, forgiven, pardoned, the weight of sin lifted off carried away by Christ the One to whom she is betrothed. Not stopping here, in the classic words of any respectable infomercial, but wait there's more!

Shunem is said to be the same as Shuni, which interestingly means quiet or to rest. Shulamite then describes one who has or will enter into His rest as Hebrews chapters 3 and 4 describe. But most importantly we see not only is His name given to the Bride, not only is she called by His name, not only is it upon her, it is within her! *(Galatians 3:27; Colossians 1:27)*. Keep in mind a name carries authority.

The Cry and Acceptance of the Bride

Again however this is not the person to whom we are first introduced, no. Who we see in the beginning is a person in desperation, one bound and in need of deliverance. She cries: "Let Him kiss me with the kisses of His mouth." This word kiss, which we will look at in more detail later, is an important one in meaning. First it carries the meaning to be armed, equipped, attached to, and touched by, and two it comes from a word meaning to burn. So as our story begins we see the exhortation of the one who has encountered the source of life, hope, peace, redemption, and salvation and recognizes her need to be joined with and touched by this King of Kings. It is His kiss and His touch that will not only arm and equip her but will also kindle a fire of purification and passion within her.

The kiss of His mouth is His word and all that His Word encompasses both given to and spoken to us. It is His breath, His Spirit as the mouth by definition is the means of blowing, the breath of life, the very breath that gave Adam, the man of dust life and intimate relationship with God.

In Scripture we also see that a kiss was a mark of reconciliation *(Genesis 33:4, 2 Samuel 14:33)*. It is His life given to and for His Church that causes our spirit to live again, allowing us to once again be united with and live in the presence God. We need His life and His Word released into our soul if we are to be equipped for the battles we face and if we are to walk in His presence. His kiss is His giving unto His Bride His Spirit, uniting Himself with His Bride.

The permission for His Kiss and intimate touch, and for Him to have personal access to her heart and soul is hers to give. She must desire, accept, and allow it. The Kiss, the beginning of intimacy, is the opening of the door of our heart to experience intimacy and relationship with Jesus beyond that offered by traditional man-made religion. It is an offer of relationship that transcends mere intellectual, theoretical, and philosophical knowledge about Jesus, which often serve only to preserve the separation between God and Man. Intimacy is the all-out access of the Bridegroom, Jesus and the Bride, Church to one another, a relationship that delights in the restoration of the communion between God and Man. Perhaps Job described it best after his personal encounter with God: Before I knew You, when all the knowledge I had was what someone else had told me, I spoke of that which was beyond my understanding but now that I have seen You and experienced You, I now know how wrong I was about You *(Job 42)*.

> *Matthew 11:28–29 (KJV)*
> *28 Come unto me, all ye that labour and are heavy laden, and I will give you rest. 29 Take my yoke upon you, and learn of me; for I am meek and lowly in heart: and ye shall find rest unto your souls.*

Having received His kiss, we hear the Bride cry in Song 1:4: "Lead me or *Draw* me Away." As Hosea said, The Lord brings

Himself down to our level drawing us gently and affectionately lifting away our burdens. Not as slaves but as sons, not forcing us, but giving us the opportunity to follow Him voluntarily *(Hosea 11:4; John 6:35, 44, 12:32).* The principle of the dispensation of Grace is summed up in this phrase "lead or draw me away" as it indicates her willingness, her choice to submit, surrender, obey, and follow Him. The day approaches in which there will be no such option, as He will rule and judge with a rod of iron, a day in which every knee will be made to bow.

Draw also means to develop; our response to Jesus must be that we desire Him to lead us, teach us, and develop us in the deeper knowledge of His love for us as He takes us into His secret place. Examining *Hosea 11:4* we see when God draws with love He heals, sustains, and removes the yoke of oppression and bondage. As the Bride recognizes the anointed king and His love for her She knows He has the desire and the authority to take her away, delivering her from the life she has been living. As He calls and leads with a gentle loving voice, Jesus reveals how precious we are to Him and how He longs for relationship and communion. He longs to give His Bride the peace she so greatly needs and desires. He leads by peace, He guides by peace, and no matter what the circumstances, trials, or troubles we face in life, in Jesus peace is made available *(Isaiah 55:12; Luke 1:79; John 16:33).* The peace we access as we make the step toward sanctification.

As the Bride is drawn away and removed from the vineyards of her oppressive brothers we begin to discover the idea of sanctification, as *2 Corinthians 6:14–17* says, "Come out from…and be separate. A Bride must separate herself from her past life, coming under a new authority as stated in *Psalm 45:10–11.*

> *Psalm 45:10–11 (KJV)*
> *10 Hearken, O daughter, and consider, and incline thine ear; forget also thine own people, and thy father's house; 11 So shall the king greatly desire thy beauty: for he is thy Lord; and worship thou him.*

Here the Psalmist instructs the bride to cut off old loyalties, old lifestyles, and anything that competes with this new life. As we will see in *Song 2:15* the Bride must seek to overcome the daily distractions that seek to interfere in their relationship. As she is brought into "His Chambers," we see one of Satan's primary attacks against this intimacy, condemnation! Coming into His holy presence, she has the sudden sense that she is unworthy of the King.

A Bride Called out of Darkness

In *Song 1:5* she proclaims: "I am Dark, but lovely." Jesus, the Bridegroom, calls those dwelling in darkness, those without peace into His presence *(1 Peter 2:9)*. Dark but lovely on the surface describes suntanned women of that day, unlike fair skinned women in the King's chambers they were often mere slave laborers working in the fields. But at a deeper level, dark but lovely describes the person who recognizes the need for and the acceptance of Christ. It is the person recognizing their own righteousness is but filthy rags. "Don't look at me" is often our reaction when we sense the presence of Jesus, just as Isaiah we feel unworthy and unfit for the king. As Isaiah said:

> *Isaiah 6:5 (KJV)*
> *5 Then said I, Woe is me! for I am undone; because I am a man of unclean lips, and I dwell in the midst of a people of unclean lips: for mine eyes have seen the King, the Lord of hosts.*

In *Song 1:5* she compares herself to the tents of Kedar. In *Psalm 120* we find a key to understanding this metaphor.

> *Psalm 120:1–7 (KJV)*
> *Plea for Relief from Bitter Foes*
> *In my distress I cried unto the Lord, and he heard me. 2 Deliver my soul, O Lord, from lying lips, and from a deceitful tongue. 3 What shall be*

*given unto thee? or what shall be done unto thee, thou false tongue? 4 Sharp arrows of the mighty, with coals of juniper. 5 Woe is me, that I sojourn in Mesech, that I dwell in the tents of **Kedar**! 6 My soul hath long dwelt with him that hateth peace. 7 I am for peace: but when I speak, they are for war.*

Kedar is a word meaning dark, dusk, from a word meaning to mourn, darkness, and sorrow. Darkness as we also know refers a lack of light, or truth, thus the Bride is one delivered from deception, darkness, lies; she is free from slavery, free to worship Him, free from anxiety or lack of peace. *Ezekiel 27:13; 32:18, 26; 38:2–3 39:1* paints the picture, as does *Psalm 120*, of Mesehch as warring, terroristic, enslavers of men, pagan, worldly, evil, those appointed to God's judgment. Mesehch symbolizes those outside of covenant with God. *Psalm 120* is a psalm of a homesick person who has been living in the midst of the enemies camp, a pilgrim, a stranger in the land of a people who know not the Lord, living as it were amongst those who hate and persecute, just as the true Christian in our World today. Light and darkness do not co-exist; they do not mix with one another. Therefore there is this warring or lack of peace because the true Bride will not compromise his or her faith or faithfulness to the Lord *(2 Corinthians 6:14, 1 John 2:15)* thus making her the enemy of those in the land in which she dwells.

Though she sees herself as dark; Jesus sees her differently. Our beauty, our value to Him is not what we possess, not about our gifts or talents, not what we have or have not done, how we look, or any other natural standard of measure, it is in who we are in Him. We are His creation originally made in His image, created for fellowship with Him. So immeasurable is His valuation of this fellowship that He was willing to step out of heaven and become one of us in order to lay down His life paying the price required to redeem that relationship. This is where the Bride finds her true worth and value.

In Him we are made fair and clean, in Him we have been made fit and worthy," Indeed, what He has done has made us righteous, worthy once again to have fellowship with God, worthy again to be called His sons and daughters. He sees us as pure and undefiled. To His Bride He says "you are beautiful, there is no flaw in you, everything about you is beautiful, there is nothing wrong or shameful with you at all *(Song 4:7)*." Jesus has cleansed His Church; He has sanctified His Bride making her holy without sin *(Ephesians 5:25–27)*.

Sadly however, many of us face a recurring battle to overcome the sense of un-worthiness and condemnation. Though there be nothing good in the flesh the fact remains there is no condemnation to those who are in Christ *(Romans 7:18, 8:1)*. There is a battle within us in relation to who we were verses who we now are. No longer are we under condemnation. Condemnation is the accusing voice of the enemy; it is that voice of judgment and the sense of guilt meant to keep us distant from Jesus. Condemnation says we deserve punishment; its purpose is to lay a burden of shame and reproach upon the Bride. Yet we must understand Jesus took not only our punishment but also our guilt and shame.

Conviction, or as some might prefer to say, convincing of righteousness can and will be a part of life in order to make aware of that which displeases the Lord, those things that hinder or cause the relationship to suffer in order for us to take responsibility and make necessary adjustments. However, we need not submit to condemnation; it is not from the Lord. Condemnation's goal is to separate us from the Lord; it is destructive. Conviction on the other hand will actually draw us to a place of obedience and we know from *John 15:14–15* that obedience leads to revelation, revelation only available in His secret place, in His chambers.

His Chambers

In Song 1:4 she says: *the King has brought me into His chambers.* Chambers refer to the secret place, the Holy of Holies. In *Psalm 91* we see the secret place is our place of protection, our refuge, the place where He covers us. It is then the place where we are alone with The Lord, a place accessible only by the blood of Jesus who has made the way open. It is a place reserved for those in covenant relationship with Christ.

> *Hebrews 10:19–20 (AMP)*
> *19 Therefore, brethren, since we have full freedom and confidence to enter into the [Holy of] Holies [by the power and virtue] in the blood of Jesus, 20 By this fresh (new) and living way which He initiated and dedicated and opened for us through the separating curtain (veil of the Holy of Holies), that is, through His flesh,*

In the secret place we become intimate with Jesus. As *Matthew 6:6* illustrates what is done in secret will be manifest publicly, seen in a good sense, when you spend time in the secret place with Jesus; His Word, Wisdom, Power, and Glory will be upon you. Like Moses whose face radiated after his experience in God's presence, through intimacy the Bride too will reflect the glory of the Lord.

Another benefit of intimacy with Jesus is found in *Ephesians 1:17–18* and *Psalm 25*.

> *Ephesians 1:17–18 (AMPC)*
> *[For I always pray to] the God of our Lord Jesus Christ, the Father of glory, that He may grant you a spirit of wisdom and revelation [of insight into mysteries and secrets] in the [deep and intimate] knowledge of Him, 18 By having the eyes of your heart flooded with light, so that you can know and understand the hope to which He has called you, and how rich is His glorious inheritance in the saints (His set-apart ones),*

Revelation knowledge, God revealing His mysteries and the secrets of covenant are the product of a deep intimate relationship. *Psalm 25* speaks of the Secrets of the Lord. When you know God's secret things you know His covenant and His counsel. This intimacy will bring you to the place of knowing and understanding His purpose and will in the earth and for your life. The first revelation we notice is the Bride now understands she is free; she has a new life, and an abundance of blessing at her disposal.

The Bridegroom King

The King in our Song is of course Jesus, the King of Kings and the Lord of Lords, the Good Shepherd, the Bridegroom *(Revelation 17:14, John 10:1–18; Matthew 9:15)*. As revealed in the Parable of the Landowner, He is the Son sent to His Father's vineyard, the One rejected and put to death by those to whom it was leased in order that they might steal the inheritance, ownership, and authority over *(Mark 12:1-12)*. Looking ahead to *Song of Solomon 8:11-12* we see clearly that all along this vineyard belongs to the King and of which we, His Church, will inherit our portion *(Acts 26:18; Ephesians 1:11)*. So plainly does this parable describe the world, the very world Jesus, the Wisdom and Word of God created, the world He upholds by His power, the world over which He delegated unto Man authority, knowing full well Man would rebel and forfeit that authority to Satan, the one whose desire is to ascend to and possess the Throne of Christ.

Love Better than Wine

The love of this King is better than wine. Scripturally, wine is something that can be used for good or bad, negative or positive. Wine is used for refreshment, celebration, rejoicing, and as the Psalmist said: to make glad the heart. Proverbs says wine takes away bitterness, misery, grief, and sorrow. Yet more and better than anything wine or this world has to offer is God's love. His love is a love stronger than death, it is more healing, more refreshing, more effective, more needed, and more desirable than anything one could ask or imagine, yet we often do not recognize this fact; sadly many cannot believe or accept it, therefore they miss out on its blessing *(Psalm 104:14; Proverbs 31:6).*

His Kiss

> *Song of Songs 1:2 (KJV)*
> *The Shulamite*
> *2 Let him kiss me with the kisses of his mouth: for thy love is better than wine.*

As we were introduced to the Bride she mentioned His kiss; again this includes His Spirit and His Word given unto us. Reading *Genesis 2:7 and 7:22* we see the life force in man is the Lord's breath or as rendered in Hebrew *ruach (roo'-akh)* "Spirit." From this Hebrew word comes the name Holy Spirit *(see Psalm 51:11).* Although the Hebraic word breath in *Genesis 1:2* differs from that found in *Genesis 2:7* the point is clear especially in light of *Genesis 7:22*, God breathed into the man He had formed, and by God's Spirit man was made to live. It is His Spirit, His Breath, that gives us life *(John 6:63; 1 Corinthians 15:45)* not only that but as a portion of our inheritance, eternal life.

> *Romans 8:10–11 Complete Jewish Bible (CJB)*
> *10 However, if the Messiah is in you, then, on the one hand, the body is dead because of sin; but, on the other hand, the Spirit is giving life because God considers you righteous. 11 And if the Spirit of the One who raised Yeshua from the dead is living in you, then the One who raised the Messiah Yeshua from the dead will also give life to your mortal bodies through his Spirit living in you.*

Kiss in this stanza is the Hebrew verb *nashaq* in the Qal imperfect form. In such form it can express an incomplete or future action, one that is past, present, future, ongoing, or conditional. As with Jesus, it is yesterday, today, and forever. *Nashaq* can also indicate a customary habit, obligation, or possibility. The Lord longs to touch, kiss, empower and equip His Bride if only we will allow Him. He longs for her passion and desire for Him to be as great as His is for Her.

Getting back to the idea of life, I came upon some very interesting commentary and meanings of the Hebrew words used in this passage. Word for word this can become very interesting, for one, it can state *"let him give me drink" in particular from the breast.* How so? One Hebrew name for God is **EL SHADDAI**: God Almighty or "God All Sufficient." "MANY BREASTED ONE" mentioned in *Genesis 49:25 (Genesis 17:1, 28:3, 35:11, including references in Job, Ruth, and Psalms).* The understanding being God is the source of all sufficiency, nourishment, and blessing. Isaiah 66:13 speaks of this aspect of God as one who comforts, as a mother comforts. However, in *Psalm 91* El Shaddai is the destroyer of enemies including: worry, fear, danger, or threat. The understanding then of El Shaddai and to be kissed by or to drink from Jesus is to access and receive from the source of all sufficiency, to receive nourishment, blessing, protection, and comfort. All we need for the sustaining of life. I would add, some scholars believe this is a reference to God giving us drink from His Word, the two Testaments of our Bible, for as Jesus said: come to me all who thirst, He is the living water forever satisfying the true needs of the soul and life. *John 6&7*

We know of course that in the context of Song of Solomon we speak of passion and love. Thus keeping in context with the Hebraic root of Kiss, *identical with nasaq*, it means to catch fire, kindle, or burn. A kiss as we know can both ignite and be a demonstration of passion. But before delving deeper into *Nashaq* in *Song 1:2* we must keep in mind some important aspects a kiss represents in Scripture; and that is a Kiss is a symbol of forgiveness, reconciliation, or restoration of relationship *(Genesis 33:4; 2 Samuel 14:33)*. And is a symbol of favor, reverence (respect), and to signify humble submission (worship) *(Psalm 2:10–12)*.

The Words used in *Song of Solomon 1:2* are:

Kisses, *neshiqah (nesh-ee-kaw)* the noun, derived from the verb *nashaq,* kiss meaning:

- To Arm Men (*literally or figuratively* to equip with military weapons) *see 1 Chronicles 12:2 and 2 Chronicles 17:17*
- To Rule
- To Touch *see Ezekiel 3:13 of wings of cherubim, gently touching each other*

It includes the idea of

- Attachment, fastening together, (to connect or join together), to embrace

So as our story began we saw the words of the one who had encountered the source of life, hope, peace, and salvation (reconciliation) and recognized her need to be joined with and touched by this King of Kings. It is His kiss and His touch that will restore, rewrite, make new, heal, and make her whole. His kiss will arm and equip her and likewise kindle a fire of purification, passion, and desire within her. The Lord watches for the smallest of hint of desire to which He may respond. That hint is of course our Kiss, our response to Him.

It is our worship:

- Submission
- Obedience
- Faith to receive by believing and trusting Him and His Word
- Thanksgiving and Praise

The Bride spoke of the kiss of His mouth. Again, the mouth by definition is the instrument of speech, commands, and blowing or *"Breath."* From God's mouth come His Spirit and His Word. Jesus's kiss is His giving unto His Bride His Spirit thus uniting Himself with

His Bride. This is one reason I think we repeatedly see in the Song *(2:7; 3:5, 10; 5:8; 8:4)* the statement "Do not stir up nor awaken love until it pleases" as this level of relationship, true love and intimacy is not forced rather it must be desired; it can only be achieved by a voluntary surrendering, submission, and giving of oneself. We must desire to be drawn away by His love.

His Kiss is His breath, His Spirit, the breath of life, the very breath, or Kiss of God's mouth that gave Adam, the man of dust, life and intimate relationship with God making Adam a living expression of God. Jesus has given His Bride/Church His Word, His Spirit, Himself and we are to be the living expression of Christ in the world! It was His life given to and for His Church that caused our spirit to live again, allowing us to once again be united with and live in the presence God and His presence to dwell within us. It is His Spirit and His Word released into our souls that equip us as His Church for the battles we face in this world.

Jesus said in:

> *Matthew 4:4 (KJV)*
> *4 But he answered and said, It is written, Man*
> *shall not live by bread alone, but by every word that*
> *proceedeth out of the mouth of God."[Deut. 8:3]*

His Kiss is His Word and all that His Word encompasses both given and spoken to us. The word of the King is power and authority, what He decrees must be done or become. This is so important when we read in the Song His words regarding the Bride, how He defines and describes her, for it is who she is and is to become. As *Psalm 45:2* says they are full of favor, grace, mercy, and compassion. Words coming from the mouth are verbal expressions of that which is in the heart and soul of man. In the context of God that would mean His Word is the expression of His heart and will through His Spirit. Although necessary for existence Man cannot survive solely on ordinary food or that which satisfies and sustains the flesh and the natural intellect. We must receive the instruction and guidance of the Holy Spirit. We cannot simply feed the natural mind; Adam and

Eve attempted to do so and they perished, they fell into deception and so do we when we lack spiritual understanding. Without God's Spirit and Word we are weak and vulnerable to the deceptions and attack of the enemy. His Spirit of Truth and Wisdom in us, and His Word, are that which arm and equip His Bride. Through the agent of Holy Spirit the Church is equipped with the weapons described in *Ephesians 6:10–18*. These weapons, the instruments of our warfare, are the imparted ability from the Lord released to His Bride not for battle against people but against principalities, against powers, against the rulers of the darkness of this age, against spiritual hosts of wickedness in the heavenly places.

God's Wisdom, these weapons, empower the Church with the strength, power, and might of the Lord enabling Her to stand prepared to oppose and overcome the systems, strategies, attacks, and deception of the devil. Foremost being the Armor of God, which is truth. As we see in *Romans 13:12* it is the armor of light; Christ is the light The Truth which exposes darkness for what it is! He has armed and equipped His Church with righteousness, the gospel of peace, peace meaning among other things to be joined together, restored, and wholeness. His Bride is armed with faith that enables her to quench all the fiery darts (attacks, lies) of the wicked one, with salvation (rescue, deliverance, and safety from destruction), with the sword of the Spirit (the Word of God) our offensive weapon, and the power of prayer and supplication in the Spirit.

His kiss is an expression of His love, "A love better than wine." Wine, as previously stated, in *Psalm 104:15 and Proverbs 31:6–7* that makes glad "the heavy heart" of one ready to perish, so that he "remembers his misery no more." Clearly Solomon speaks of a drink which satisfies the soul. Remember Jesus said to the thirsty in *John 7:37–39*, come to me and drink. So His Word and His Spirit are better, more precious, pleasing, and satisfying than anything this world has to offer able to truly make us well, joyful, and happy. Still, if we are to drink of Him, if we are to receive His kiss, we must kiss Him in return.

We saw that Kiss included the meanings of *touch and to worship.*

Luke 8:46
> *46 But Jesus said, "Somebody touched Me, for
> I perceived power going out from Me."*

When we read in the Gospels of those Jesus touched or those who touched Him we see they were cleansed, healed, made whole by His power released. Our touch, our kiss, is our worship. At least 60 times in the New Testament a Greek word meaning to kiss is used to define worship, to bow down or prostrate oneself in reverence. This touch is one we give and receive through worship, in particular passionate worship, which will result in dramatic changes in the Bride, especially in the area of her self-image.

Amended Rewritten: A New Self Image

In the Song of Solomon we see how the Bride defined herself, how others have defined her, and how He defines her. "I am dark but lovely—my own vineyard I have not kept." As she first encounters this Bridegroom she becomes fully aware of her inadequacies, shortfalls, and failures. She is conscious of what she lacks and where she has failed to perform. She is reminded of her inabilities, areas in which she is powerless, helpless, and hopeless. Ever aware of her insufficiencies and how she is unfit and unsuitable for Him. In her current status she is incompatible and inappropriate for the King. She is dark but lovely, like the tents of Kedar. Beautiful perhaps in outwardly appearance, but when He looks into her heart she cries do not look, don't judge me, If you only knew from where I have come, my abusive past. She feels, like much of the Church and those proclaiming to be Christians today, that she does not deserve His love; after all, she has done nothing to earn it.

When she looks into the mirror she has, as we now refer to it, "A Victim Mentality." She speaks of the abuse she endured by the hand of her brothers. She is ever conscious of her past, even current hurt, pain, and bondage to their will. But she is about to encounter freedom and healing by being able to walk away, letting it all go, giving it all to Him. Nevertheless, perhaps a bit confused even ashamed of her current position, status, and condition, deep within herself she recognizes she is lovely, and beautiful. She realizes this relationship may be possible after all!

This nameless somewhat nondescript Bride who like all of us started out in a condition of darkness is transformed by Christ both instantly and by process into a new person. Like Saul who became Paul, we as signified by means of Baptism, must let the past "me" be and remain crucified with Christ. As she gives it all, the pain, shame, guilt, and condemnation to the Bridegroom we see the King name and define her. He purifies her heart. She is made like wool and like the lilies, pure and white as snow.

She who considered herself black as the tents of Kedar, for indeed she was as black is that which reflects no light. She was not at that moment in her life a reflection of Him. She was absent of reflection because in her was an absence of light. Yet when she begins to follow Him, He defines her as White, White that "color" which is a complete reflector of light, reflecting back all the spectrum of light, in other words she is now a reflection of Him and Truth[1]. *Jonathan Cahn*

She is white like the lily because she is no longer self-absorbed she has given it all to Him, she is no longer dark because she no longer retains her sin, her past, her failures, her hurts and pains. Her beauty is like that of the moon, she may be scared, wounded, and have imperfections yet beautiful because she has become a reflection of Him and not of herself. *Song 6:10*

Her Reproach has been taken away. In Isaiah 4:1 we see:

> *Isaiah 4:1 (KJV)*
> *And in that day seven women shall take hold of one man, saying, We will eat our own bread, and wear our own apparel: only let us be called by thy name, to take away our reproach.*

Reproach in Hebrew can refer to disgrace, shame, guilt; it can include widowhood, barrenness, and injuries. Here we are reminded of

Ruth our first example of the Gentile Bride brought into the covenant of God. When we are called by Jesus name, the name in which resides all power, the name to which everything must bow and submit we carry the authority of Jesus name with the same right to use it, as did the Disciples. The name and authority by which they healed the sick, restored people to wholeness, cast out demons, and so much more all to His glory. All because of who He is and what He has done for us.

Her reproach taken away, His Bride-Church is clean, pure and holy in *Song. 4:7* and *6:9* He exclaims: there is no flaw in you, undefiled and perfect nothing at all wrong with you.

> *Ephesians 5:27 (KJV)*
> *27 That he might present it to himself a glorious church, not having spot, or wrinkle, or any such thing; but that it should be holy and without blemish.*

The pursuit of holiness, sanctification, is the proper response to the offer and acceptance of betrothal and must be the goal of the Bride. To more and more, day by day be conformed to and bear the image of the Lord. The very image Adam and Eve forfeited once again made possible in Christ; we, like the Bride in Song of Solomon, must relinquish the image imposed upon us taking upon ourselves His character and likeness.

As His spirit and His Word are given to and received by the Bride, His name is likewise given unto her. "Your name is ointment poured forth." He is willing to give His name, putting it upon those willing to receive it.

His Name

Your Name Is as Ointment or Oil Poured Forth

Just as an Olive must be crushed in order to release its oil, Jesus, on the night He took upon Himself the sin of the world, in His moment of suffering, under such tremendous stress prayed: if possible take "this cup" from Me. This event as we know occurred in the place called Gethsemane, which translates place of crushing, or pressing of oil *(Matthew 26:36+)*. Just as Isaiah prophesied in chapter 53 verses 5 and 10, The Messiah was bruised for our iniquities and that it pleased the Lord to bruise Him. The word translated bruise here, in the Hebrew, means to crush. This is of particular importance because His name, The Christ "Christos," in Hebrew Masciach "Messiah," as seen in *John 1:41, Daniel 9:25,* and *Isaiah 61:1* means anointed, the one anointed with oil, or *The Anointed One.* Jesus was, as *Isaiah 11:2* and *John 1:32–33* confirm, anointed with the Holy Spirit.

As Mary poured the oil of great price upon the head of Jesus its fragrance filling the house, Jesus said this anointing with costly oil signified the pouring out of His life for our salvation. After His crushing, Jesus then poured out His Spirit, the Holy Spirit, upon His Church whereby we now carry the very anointing He possessed in order to minister to a suffering world *(Acts 2:33; Titus 3:5–6)*.

He Was Poured Out

As we read In *Song 1:3* His name is ointment poured out or in the context emptied out. He emptied Himself to become a man and give His life that we might live. His name poured out signifying Jesus, our King, our Bridegroom, would be poured out as offering, the sacrifice for our redemption. His Spirit likewise poured out upon those who accept Him *(Acts 2:33, 10:45; Titus 3:6)*. We are able to emit the fragrances of Christ (which we will look into) because He poured Himself out as an offering for His Bride-Church.

Matthew 1:16 reveals His Name to be Jesus, who is called Christ "the Anointed One," (Hebrew, "Messiah"). *Daniel 9:26* prophesied of Him as "Messiah who will be cut off, but not for Himself." Cut off, crucified, He made himself an offering for our righteousness and sanctification, redeeming and purchasing for himself we His Bride, a Bride who not only receives the blessings of His name but the authority to use it to bless others and overcome the power of Satan.

Jesus is the costly oil poured forth whose name refreshes, heals, and strengthens, the oil of joy and gladness *(Psalm 45:7–8)*. The name that heals the broken heart, liberates those bound and imprisoned, that brings comfort to those in sorrow, gives joy where there was once devastation, distress, and sorrow, conquers the darkness of depression, makes righteous, and causes His Bride to bring Glory to the Lord *(Isaiah 61:1–3; Luke 4:18)*. It is the very name by which the Father receives us into His family and presence or as The Bride said into His chambers.

His desire is for man to have free access to His Most Holy Place. His desire for you is far greater than most Christians understand or comprehend. He is ready to reveal Himself to His Bride, to reveal His power, His glory, His secret counsel, and the depths of knowledge of His Word. He has revealed His name, the very name that we now bear so that we might be a light that reveals Him to others.

His Name Is the Oil of Anointing

Song of Solomon 1:3 (NKJV)
3 Because of the fragrance of your good oint-
ments, Your name is ointment poured forth...

What does she reveal when she speaks of the fragrance of His name and His name is ointment poured forth? His name Jesus, *"Yehoshua or Yeshua"* means the LORD is salvation and Christ or Messiah *"Mashiach"* His title, means the Anointed One. As we see here His name is poured out as Ointment or in Hebrew *"shemen"* *(sheh'-men)* the anointing oil, from the root *"shaman"* referring to a liquid such as from the olive, often perfumed, used not only for anointing of kings, priest, and anything sanctified to God, was also used medicinally.

What is also important to notice is that the root word for ointment is *"shem"* which is translated name. So His name is the anointing oil. Note in particular the ingredients of the anointing Oil Moses was instructed to compound in Exodus.

Exodus 30:22–25 (KJV)
The Holy Anointing Oil
   22 Moreover the Lord spake unto Moses, saying,
   23 Take thou also unto thee principal spices, of pure myrrh five hundred shekels, and of sweet cinnamon half so much, even two hundred and fifty shekels, and of sweet Calamus (sweet-smelling cane) two hundred and fifty shekels, 24 And of cassia five hundred shekels, after the shekel of the sanctuary, and of oil olive an hin: 25 And thou shalt make it an oil of holy ointment, an ointment compound after the art of the apothecary: it shall be an holy anointing oil.

Notice also in *Psalm 45:7–8* when speaking prophetically of Jesus, the Bridegroom King, that He is anointed with the oil of joy and gladness, and that the smell of His garments emit the fragrance of the Holy Anointing Oil. Also note His fragrance in *Song 3:6.* When we compare this to the fragrance of the Bride in *Song of Solomon 4:13–14* we see she is anointed with His anointing, giving off His fragrance, just as "The Church" does of Christ as seen in *2 Corinthians 2:14–16.* Oil is a symbol of the Holy Spirit and it is through Holy Spirit that the fragrance of Christ is transferred upon and released through the believer. We, His Bride, are His fragrance both to the Father and the World.

2 Corinthians 2:14–16 (NKJV)
   14 Now thanks be to God who always leads us in triumph in Christ, and through us diffuses the fragrance of His knowledge in every place. 15 For we are to God the fragrance of Christ among those who are being saved and among those who are perishing. 16 To the one we are the aroma of death leading to death, and to the other the aroma of life leading to life...

As indicated by this passage Paul explains that the fragrance of Christ within the believer will release the Knowledge of Christ into the world. It will be unto the world "life leading to life" or "death leading to death" to those who perceive it. Those responding to the Holy Spirit will be drawn into a relationship with Christ. Those rejecting the light of His truth for darkness will find Christ fragrance repulsive and repugnant.

Consider again the fragrance of the oil Mary poured on the feet of Jesus anointing Him for burial as mentioned in *John 12:1–7*, a fragrance that filled the house infusing everyone present with its scent. We the Bride diffuse His fragrance because we are made one with Christ *(1 Corinthians 6:17)*, and as *Romans 6* teaches our old nature was crucified and died with Christ, and as symbolized by baptism, buried and resurrected into newness of life in Him.

Earlier we spoke of His Kiss, His Breath. Notice in *Song 7:8* that the King likens her breath to that of apples, and in *Song 2:3* she describes the King as an apple tree, the fruit of which she has partaken of and been refreshed. He is the fragrance that she emits; she is filled with His Spirit *(Luke 5:37–39, Acts 2; Ephesians 5:18)*. His Spirit is that which flows from within the Bride. *1 Corinthians 6:17* explains why her breath and His are the same.

> *1 Corinthians 6:17 (NKJV)*
> *17 But he who is joined to the Lord is one spirit with Him.*

She has partaken of Him in intimacy and communion; as indicated in the word refresh she is comforted and supported, some of the very blessings we in fact receive from the Holy Spirit.

The Place of His Name

The Lord builds a house, His family, and a place for His Name to inhabit. Where the Lord places His name is the place He dwells, inhabits, and abides *(Deuteronomy 12:5, 26:2)*.

David was promised his heir would build a house for the throne and name of the Lord. Solomon built a physical structure where God promised to place His name, His heart, and His eyes forever *(2 Chronicles 2:4; 7:16)*. Of course we now understand that the prophecy to David that his son Solomon would build the temple is of deeper context and intimated that Jesus would build His Church, the temple of the Holy Spirit, His family and dwelling place, the place God's name, heart, eyes, and His presence to eternally remain *(1 Kings 5:5; 1 Kings 9:3; 1 Corinthians 6:19; 2 Corinthians 6:16)*. Where the Lord places His name there is His presence. His eyes and heart are upon the place His name resides. We can say it this way: His attention and concern, His focus, His thoughts, His consideration, His affection are directed toward the place of His name. We as His Bride are important to Jesus; He has made Himself to be responsible for His Bride. He has made Himself to be the carrier of the burdens of His Bride. All of which He is able to do if we allow Him to do so by our surrender.

Receiving His Name

Jew or Gentile, whoever calls upon, that is invokes and worships, whoever accepts His name shall receive His name, His salvation, life, and become a child of God *(Romans 10:13; Acts 15:14; John 20:31)*. Whoever has His name, and is baptized in His name has forgiveness for their sins, is justified, sanctified, and pure in the Father's eyes, and receives the gift of the Holy Spirit *(Acts 2:38; 1 Corinthians 6:11)*. Greatest of all is those who have His name, have submitted to His name and His authority, and His discipline will one day see Him face to face.

To be called by the name means you belong to Jesus, you have entered into covenant with Him. You have dedicated or sanctified yourself unto Him. When one takes the Name of Jesus it is in order to bring glory and honor to Christ, it is to come under His authority, it is to abide in Him and Him in you, it is to bear his name by supporting His doctrine, ideals, and advancing His Kingdom by becoming His witness. It is to be wholly His, and being transformed into his likeness. It is to as He states in *Revelation 2:13* holding fast to His name, remaining faithful, obedient to His word, and submitted to His authority no matter what the consequence.

Transformed can be further understood when we examine "Name" in Greek. HELPS Word-studies says the transliterated Greek word *ónoma* refers to the manifestation or revelation of someone's character. And according to Hebrew notions, a name is inseparable from the person to whom it belongs, it is something of their essence and is synonymous with their authority. In the Old Covenant's culture and society a person's name represented the person, it described who they were, and it represented the authority of that person. Concerning the name of God, God's name is then the manifestation or expression of the nature and character of God. All that belongs to Jesus, His nature (qualities, identity, spirit), character, and all His name encompasses are given to and put upon His Bride through and in His name. His name is Wonderful, Counselor, Mighty God, Everlasting Father, and Prince of Peace *(Revelation 19:16; Isaiah 9:6)*. And for example, His name is Yahweh Rapha, The Lord our Healer, our name then becomes as in my case, Mike The Healed, and so forth. Jesus name is the Word of God and Jesus is and has always been God, the light and life of man *(Revelation 19:13; John 1:1–5)*. Jesus said in *John 20:31* Life is in His name. What is Life? *John 17:3* says it is to know God, His person, character, authority, and power.

The Right to Use His Name

Noteworthy is that in Biblical times sons were given the authority of their father's name and commissioned to act on behalf their father. When you receive Jesus's name you receive rights, and authority to use and possess everything that belongs to that name. Jesus said: "all authority (power) belongs to Him *(Matthew 28:18)*. The role of the Bride of Jesus is to continue the ministry of Christ through the empowerment and gifts of the Holy Spirit by being a witness of Christ and reflecting Jesus, bringing glory to His name. As the Bride is called by His name, we are empowered with His authority by the Holy Spirit *(Acts 1:8; John 14:12)*.

In marriage the Bride receives the name of her husband, in such she inherits the rights and privileges of that name in particular the authority of that name. Jesus we know has given His Bride, The Church, His name and the authority of His name. With His name comes His power. And as "The Church" becomes one with Jesus, she takes on the character and characteristics of Jesus. In fact the term Christian was first used to indicate those who followed and acted like Christ. Our name then is who we are, it is our identity, and our identity is His identity. By His name we know who we are and the authority and power we possess. Remember in *John 14:26* the Holy Spirit, who is the representation of Jesus and His power, was sent in His Name. So too, all that is in His name is in us!

Again, with His name comes His power, as Jesus said: "In my name you will…"

> *Mark 16:17–18 (AMP)*
> *17 And these attesting signs will accompany those who believe: in My name they will drive out demons; they will speak in new languages; 18 They will pick up serpents; and [even] if they drink anything deadly, it will not hurt them; they will lay their hands on the sick, and they will get well.*

> *John 14:12–14 (AMP)*
> *12 I assure you, most solemnly I tell you, if anyone steadfastly believes in Me, he will himself be able to do the things that I do; and he will do even greater things than these, because I go to the Father. 13 And I will do [I Myself will grant] whatever you ask in My Name [as presenting all that I AM], so that the Father may be glorified and extolled in (through) the Son. 14 [Yes] I will grant [I Myself will do for you] whatever you shall ask in My Name [as presenting all that I AM].*

Here we see Jesus promise to give as a gift to His Church the manifestation of the power and authority of His name and to show or make a display of that power, authority and glory. Christ the anointed one endued with the power of the Holy Spirit poured out not only Himself but also His name.

The Authority of His Name

Ephesians 1:20–23 (KJV)
20 Which he wrought in Christ, when he raised him from the dead, and set him at his own right hand in the heavenly places, 21 Far above all principality, and power, and might, and dominion, and every name that is named, not only in this world, but also in that which is to come: 22 And hath put all things under his feet, and gave him to be the head over all things to the church,
23 Which is his body, the fulness of him that filleth all in all.

God declared to the Israelites they must not use His name in vain, in emptiness of speech, lying, deceitful, or false pretense, nor make use of it for any idle, frivolous, or insincere purpose. Some of the ways we can take God's name in vain is one through hypocrisy, confessing to belong to, love, and are submitted to Jesus but not living in obedience, as *Psalm 81:15* states those who hate the Lord pretend submission to Him. Another is by breaking covenant through idolatry, unfaithfulness, and turning away from the Truth. And yet another is the unauthorized application and exploitation of the authority of His name. He is the highest and final authority, to whom all and everything must submit both in heaven, and on earth, those of flesh and those who are spirits (*Philippians 2:9–10; Luke 10:17*).

In His name, which we have been authorized to use, is the power and authority to heal and make whole *(Acts 3:6, 16; Acts 4:7, 10)*.

However, just because a person uses His name activating the authority of His name, or even proclaims to be called by His name is not a guarantee that person is submitted to Him or belongs to Him. No, it is not enough to simply know or believe in Him and the power of His name. The demons know him and His name. Satan knows Him and even believes in Him, but! Jesus plainly states there are those to whom He will say:

> *Matthew 7:21–23 (KJV)*
> *I Never Knew You*
> *21 Not every one that saith unto me, Lord, Lord, shall enter into the kingdom of heaven; but he that doeth the will of my Father which is in heaven. 22 Many will say to me in that day, Lord, Lord, have we not prophesied in thy name? and in thy name have cast out devils? and in thy name done many wonderful works? 23 And then will I profess unto them, I never knew you: depart from me, ye that work iniquity*

His desire is to give His name, for man to call upon and be called by His name, to come under His authority, for only then do we truly belong to Him. If we belong to Jesus He is our Shepherd, declaring Himself, as was prophesied by Micah, to be the Good Shepherd who gives His life for those who choose to follow Him. And those who do so will hear, recognize, and obey His voice *(Micah 5:4; John 10:1–18)*. Those called by His name, those obedient to His voice lawfully wield the authority of His name, we rule and reign with Him, we have the authority of His name now. When we are given His name, His Life, power, and His light as Jesus said in *Matthew 5:15* and *Mark 4:21–22* we cannot hide it or keep it secret. We can no longer be veiled.

Veiled

Song of Solomon 1:7(NKJV)
(To Her Beloved)
   7 Tell me, O you whom I love, where you feed
your flock, where you make it rest at noon. For why
should I be as one who veils herself by the flocks of
your companions?

As she betrothed herself to the King she entered the first phase of marriage. She comes under His authority, no longer under the power and influence of her brothers. She is to be called by a new name; she is being given a new identity afforded her by this marriage. We understand this principle from the account of Mary and Joseph. Even though only engaged, Mary had become subject to Joseph, evidenced by Joseph's authority to "put her away" when she was discovered to be pregnant *(Matthew 1:18–25)*.

We can gain a great deal of understanding concerning being veiled when we study passages such as *2 Corinthians 3:14–18, 4:3–7; Isaiah 25:7–9, 29:10–24; and Ephesians 4:18.* First we understand veiled refers to hardness of heart, ignorance, and the inability to "know" Christ or to understand truth. It is unbelief; it is blindness, which is Satan's deception of the world. Second we recognize that only Christ and His Holy Spirit can remove the veil. And we learn that when the veil is removed, the Bride is awakened to truth, she receives revelation, she is enabled to see and know the Lord. She is able in her heart and mind to understand His word. She experiences the salvation and life of the Lord being delivered from death, which is eternal separation from God. Unveiled, the Bride is set free, she is transformed into His image, and enabled to become His reflection. She is empowered to reflect His glory and release His knowledge upon those in darkness.

An unveiling has begun, The Lord, I believe is beginning to reveal His "true" Bride, everyone will soon know who this true Bride of Christ is. It will be clear for, as we will see later in this poem she

43

begins to radiate His very nature. She petitions, make it known I now belong to you! Why should it be delayed, why must I be kept a secret.

When She says Why should I be veiled we see her cry to be revealed, no longer hidden but recognized as accepted by and in covenant with the King of Kings. Be it forever known to powers of darkness that once held me under their control and influence: I am no longer subject to you! No longer must I listen to your accusations; no longer must I be ashamed, no longer will I live under guilt. No longer a subject of the kingdom of darkness for she has chosen and will forever follow the Good Shepherd.

The Good Shepherd

Shortly before she begins to recognize the King as a shepherd she proclaims "The King has brought me into His chambers *(Song 1:4, 7)*, a statement that directs our attention to Luke's account of Parable of the Lost Sheep. As Jesus is accused by the Pharisees of receiving or welcoming sinners, He indicates the type of loving shepherd He is, one who has left His place to seek out and pursue the one who is lost and gone astray, the one surrounded by the harshness and dangers of the wilderness. If she will respond and allow Him to take her she will be rescued and carried by the Shepherd; delivered from the perils of life and shadow of death she will be brought, as it were, into His banqueting House of celebration and rejoicing. This we see is the case. When asked where He feeds His flock, she has made the decision to follow Him and thereby enter into His rest. Answering His calling and offer of relationship she accepts Him as her Shepherd. The King when instructing her to follow the footsteps of the flock acknowledges that she is now accepted as His. She likewise knows she belongs to Him for she uses the word for shepherd penned in *Psalm 23* years prior by her future father-in-law King David when in *Song 2:16* she proclaims "I am His He is mine-He feeds His flock." David declaring in *Psalm 23* the Lord to be his Shepherd not only states His position he describes what the Lord-Shepherd ensures those of His flock.

David's Axiom

That the lord is David's shepherd is not based upon a mere fact or reason in the world; no, the only condition by which it rest upon, the condition making it truth is David's decision to submit to the Lord. In *Psalm 23* David poetically states this truth, and then describes the consequences resulting from that truth. These blessings and benefits belong to anyone who chooses to pasture on, or "eat of Him"; those who trust, and those listen to His voice for instruction, wisdom, guidance, and direction *(See Matthew 26:26–28; John 6:41–58)*.

In Jesus, we are led to a place of rest and provision. We are restored not only in relationship with God by being forgiven and made righteous; we are healed in both body and soul, physically, mentally, and emotionally *(1 Peter 2:24)*. We have at our disposal peace no matter how dire the circumstance. His peace is the result of His rod of authority and staff of guidance and support. Our realization of this peace is congruent to and contingent upon the degree of control He has of our life; the more submitted we are the greater our peace, strength, and comfort will be. A strength we will need to overcome the darkness surrounding us and ever at work to seduce the Church. Luke quoting the prophecy of Isaiah confirms this aspect of Christ saying:

> *Luke 1:79 (KJV)*
> *79 To give light to them that sit in darkness and in the shadow of death, to guide our feet into the way of peace.*

Jesus's Church has available, if we so choose, truth to guide us in the darkest of days when everyone and everything in the world is given over to the darkness, deception, immorality, and total confusion. Though we face trouble, trial, and tribulation, even when we are not preserved from or delivered immediately from such, we can have peace knowing He will guide us through, ever with us, always in control, leading us to ultimate victory and celebration.

His Table

Song 1:12, while He sits at His table describes His first coming to partake of that which was determined before the foundation of the world. It was love for us that He paid the price for our redemption and our healing.

The Lord has prepared for us a table in the presence of our enemies. First of all our enemy is our old adversary Satan. Enemies are also those or that which bring distress, overwhelm, harass, plague, or bind a person. They are sickness, diseases, and afflictions.

The Lord is Himself the table "meal" prepared for us in the presence of our enemy. This table is His covenant with us represented by what we now celebrate as the Lords Supper. This meal is our non-carnal weapon against these enemies. Our bread is His word; it is His stripe-laden body, the stripes that healed our sickness and diseases, making we, His Bride whole. His blood is the currency that purchased our redemption and forgiveness making His Bride righteousness, blameless, and holy. This meal represents His covenant with His Bride.

This covenant affected an exchange whereby we exchange afflictions and diseases, any area of bondage for healing, wholeness, and liberty. We exchange suffering and sorrow for His joy and peace.

The word teaches Jesus is the Bread of Life *(John 6:35)* and healing to be the children's bread *(Mark 7:26–28)*. The Lord sent His Word to heal *(Psalm 107:20)*. His Word does not return void but prospers and accomplishes that for which it was sent *(Isaiah 55:11)*. Jesus fulfilled that which was spoken by Isaiah the prophet, "He Himself took "accepted and received" our infirmities "weaknesses, illnesses," and bore "removed" our sicknesses and diseases *(Matthew 8:17)*. As we partake of this victory celebration and His merciful covenant loyalty continually pursues our defeated enemy must watch to his derision.

Our Shepherd, Our Friend

This word Shepherd also has the context of friendship and to be a companion, even best friend. In a marriage if one's spouse is not their best friend, if there is not regular open and meaningful communication through listening and talking, if there is not intimacy, there is a problem in the relationship! In *John 15:15–21*, Jesus calls those He has chosen, those who obey Him, friends. The difference between a friend and a mere acquaintance is in what you know. He reveals the secrets of the God's kingdom and covenant to those who are His friend, *Psalm 25* tells us this includes God's secret counsel. The more intimate one is with the Lord the more revelation and understanding they will receive. Yet in *John 15* we also hear Jesus say the world hates Him and those intimate with him will likewise be hated by the world. For His name's sake He will lead and guide you in righteousness for His name's sake, because of righteousness you will be hated.

Do you want to know if you truly are His Bride sincerely submitted to His authority, that you do indeed carry His name, and will dwell in His house forever? One way to be sure is that your lifestyle and opinions are so contrary to the world's that you are hated by the world. Jesus made plain that the World will hate His true Bride *(John 15:18–19; Luke 21:17)*.

CHAPTER 2
The Betrothal

Betrothed

As said the period following betrothal was a time of sanctification, the time of separation, days of preparation as we prepare ourselves for Him as He prepares a home for us.

> *Colossians 1:22 (KJV)*
> *22 In the body of his flesh through death, to present you holy and unblameable and unreprove-able in his sight:*

In the Greek, to the original audience, it would be understood that He has reconciled the Church making His Bride holy, unblemished, and irreproachable before Him. If we were to do the word study we would discover we are made blameless, without blemish, spot, or fault just as He himself is, we have been made "like Him" once again in His image, the image of God. We stand and will stand before the Lord un-accused, unaccusable, not convictable, not to be called into account for our sins, sanctified, irreproachable in His sight.

> *Ephesians 5:25–27 (KJV)*
> *25 Husbands, love your wives, even as Christ also loved the church, and gave himself for it; 26*

That he might sanctify and cleanse it with the wash-
ing of water by the word, 27 That he might present
it to himself a glorious church, not having spot, or
wrinkle, or any such thing; but that it should be
holy and without blemish.

Sanctification is holiness; the Brides beauty, which He describes, is the product of sanctification. When David said worship the Lord in the beauty of holiness, in one sense he was saying in consecration, dedication, by being set apart, or we might say by being exclusive. She is beautiful; her beauty is *spirit and truth* worship in that she is wholly devoted to the Bridegroom. In her reverence, she is the glory of her husband *(1 Corinthians 11:7)*. She is the lily among thorns.

A Lily among Thorns

Song of Solomon 2:1–2(KJV)
I am the rose of Sharon, and the lily of the
valleys.
2 As the lily among thorns, so is my love among
the daughters.

Eight times in Song of Solomon the term lily or lilies is mentioned. Beginning in chapter 2 verses 1 and 2 the statement is made: "I am the rose of Sharon, and the lily of the valleys," there is some debate as to who makes this first statement, but clearly it is He who speaks of the Bride in verse 2 describing her as a lily among thorns. It takes two or three witnesses to establish conformation, yet I propose four arguments for why in each instance it the bride spoken of as the lily. First, in *Isaiah 65:10* Sharon is referred to as a fold of flocks of sheep. Jesus said we are the sheep of His pasture and three of the six times lilies are mentioned in Song of Solomon it is in reference is to the King feeding His flock. Second, in *Hosea 14:5* the lily is used as a metaphor for Israel, God's Bride. Third, the Lily consists of six petals, six in scripture is the number for Man. Fourth, in chapter 6 we see the King return to His garden to gather His lilies.

About the Lily

The *1901 Jewish Encyclopedia* states: *The first account of the lily is given by Ibn Ezra in his commentary on the Song of Solomon "It is a white flower of sweet but narcotic perfume, and it receives its name because the flower has, in every case, six petals, within which are six long filaments." … The heart of this flower is directed upward, even though it be among thorns, thus symbolizing the trust in God which should be felt by Israel amid all afflictions…* [1]

Fausset's Bible Dictionary states: *The lily is a very noble plant in the East; it grows to a considerable height, but has a weak stem. The Church is weak in herself, yet is strong in Him that supports her*[2]. You might think the Lily being tall, beautiful, and unguarded would represent pride but in fact it is exactly opposite as we know from Genesis it is the thorn that represent pride.

The Hebrew word for Lily, *Shushan, shoshan, shoshannah, or Shoshannim*, means ornament, straight, or trumpet and interestingly comes from the Hebrew word *suws (sus or sis)*, meaning to be glad, joy, rejoice, to be bright, cheerful, and conveys the idea of whiteness. Whiteness of course refers to purity. A trumpet in Solomon's day and Biblically was not so much a musical instrument but rather an instrument for producing a noise such as an alarm, signal, announcement, or proclamation, for example a call to war, to worship, to celebration, gathering of the people, to announce the presence of the King or as with Moses on the mountain, God's presence. An ornament is something that draws attention, an accessory, in particular of worship, possessing a quality of grace, beauty, or honor. It is something that adds expressiveness in order to show, reveal, or manifest. Is this not exactly who we, Jesus's Church are and what we are to do as His witness.

Lilies and Thorns

The Lily symbolizes the Bride's sweetness, modesty, virginity, purity of heart, and true inner devotion. Like the lily, she is the image of beauty and grace in a cursed, perverse, and rebellious world. Her beauty far surpasses the thorny weeds surrounding her, as she remains pure amid evil. Yet it is not of her own power that she remains so, for she is indeed like the Lily, weak in herself yet strong in Him. Being in the open fields, exposed to many dangers and enemies, she is in need of and requires His protection to survive and overcome precarious circumstances and those who attempt to poison, hurt, and wound her. To survive, to flourish, and to be fruitful, her heart and focus must remain on the things above, on Him who sits on the throne.

From the lily we learn a great deal of who the Bride is or can be. The Lilies, Jesus said in *Matthew 6:19–34,* neither toil, laboring to the point of growing weary or exhausted by self-effort; nor spin, as in weaving fabrics to make their own garments. The obvious connotation here is to self-righteousness. It describes attempting to earn or deserve, God's grace and love or to become righteous through vain religious works. Lilies, whose wealth, glory, and honor far exceed that of Solomon's, symbolize those who, seek first, trust in, and value God's kingdom. They neither worry nor are overcome by anxiety, for they are free of fear or distrust of God. Lilies do not strive; they trust God, knowing He is responsible there for provision, protection, and clothing, in particular salvation and righteousness. Lilies represent those who are at peace and are whole. They need not be anxious, distracted, or confused; they are not divided in heart, nor double minded. They will not falter between two opinions as to which God they will serve, worship, trust, and obey *(See 1 Kings 18:21; Joshua 24:15; Matthew 6:24).*

Lilies then, symbolize those who have entered into His rest. Though vulnerable to the thorns surrounding them, often piercing, wounding, or disturbing their lives, they rest assured. Why? Lilies are open flowers; a lily then is one who is open and thus able to receive. Though at times they may bend under pressure of trial and tribulation, their hearts are directed upward, filled with faith and confidence in the Lord, in-spite of what they face, or experience they rise again and again to receive and partake of the promises of God. Only that which is open can receive. A Lily is one that simply receives.

A thorn on the other hand represents the curse and being under the curse, the curse of the ground, the toil of man. Thorns not only represent the curse, they represent man's desire to be self-sufficient, his self-will, pride, lust, man's self-effort, anything natural as the source. A Thorn is one who must work for, strive for, and earn everything through his or her own strength, talent, ability, or resources. A Thorn will take everything personal including the credit for his or her success or failure. Like Adam and Eve who brought the world under this curse, they say "I," I will make my own decisions; I will determine for myself what is good or evil, right or wrong. One who is a thorn is in essence a god to himself, one whose doctrine is relativism, one whose end is rejection, and whose destiny is the fire of judgment. *(Genesis 3:17–18; 2 Samuel 23:6–7; Hebrews 6:8).* Hardhearted and rebellious, they are guarded, closed, protective, self-persevering, untrusting, and therefore unable to receive.

Thorns, as Jesus said in "The Parable of the Soils" *(Matthew 13:7, 22)* are those possessed by the love and desire for the things and the distractions of the world. *Matthew 13:22; Luke 8:14 and Mark 4:18–19* describe thorns as cares, worries, anxieties, concerns, or divided hearts concerning things pertaining to this earthly life. Thorns are described as riches and the deceitfulness of riches, materialism, possessions, wealth, and the seduction or seducing influence of and lust for riches. Thorns are described as the pleasures of life and desires for other things. The word pleasures here in the Greek is the word from which we derive the term "hedonism," a doctrine that moral values are defined in terms of pleasures. Hedonism is the pursuit of passions through unrestrained or undisciplined sensuality, and the self-indulgent gratification of sensual or physical desires at the expense of other things. Thorns are those things Satan uses to close us off to, choke, restrict, or stop the flow of blessing from the Kingdom of God into our lives, preventing us from being fruitful.

Thorns are the world around us, the world we live and work in, the one we interact with on a daily basis, a system under the influence and control of the god of this world, Satan *(2 Corinthians 4:4)*. Thorns can be a tremendous temptation and one can easily become like the thorns. Painful as it may be, we must often, if not daily, battle with the thorns in our life.

Thorns in the Flesh

When the Apostle Paul spoke of the thorn in his flesh to what did he refer? Most of us have heard at least one preaching in which we were told it was a physical ailment. Even though the word Paul uses to describe his thorn can refer to physical sickness or the handicap associated with such, the problem with this view is that in Hebrew scripture thorns do not refer to physical ailments. Thorns do however refer to many things such as test, troubles, enemies, adversity, and adversaries. Thorns can be conflicts, temptations, grief, harassments, reproaches, persecutions, and perhaps our proclivities, character issues, weaknesses; tares if you will, in our heart that attempt to draw us away from the Lord. Often in scripture thorns are associated with traps or snares, those things that capture, bind, and hinder God's people from receiving and maintaining His purpose and blessings. The Lord cautioned the Israelites through Moses and Joshua that the ways of the godless nations they were to dispossess had the potential to turn them away from Him, being as said "thorns in their sides" that would lead to their disobedience and violation of their covenant with Him, things that would eventually rob them of their inheritance *(Joshua 23:17; Judges 1–3)*. Nevertheless, God allowed and used the "thorns" to test and discipline the heart, faithfulness, and obedience of His people.

As for the Apostle Paul, we do know Paul had some sort of problem with his eyes but was this Paul's thorn we read of in *2 Corinthians 12:7–10*, for it is true that the words Paul and Jesus use in the passage can indicate an aliment? Nonetheless, what is clear is this thorn was something in his flesh permitted by God in order to keep him humble. As we are aware, scripturally the Flesh refers to our human nature; it includes our sense and reasoning. And yes, as long as we are in this physical body, we will battle with frailties, weaknesses, even our own mortality. But Paul said his thorn was a messenger, someone or something sent of Satan to buffet him. To Buffet means to oppose, battle, beat, toss like a ship on tempestuous seas in order to knock him off course. He may have referred to something or someone in his past, or simply something he just never quite overcame in his character, we are not told for certain. What we do know is that Paul endured insults, hardships, persecutions, troubles, and suffering for the message of Christ. The point is we are Lilies among thorns, we all have thorns in our lives, some of which God allows, some God may never completely remove, those that are designed to test us, keep us humble, and to keep us reliant upon God's grace and strength and not our own. When tried or pierced by such we must remember Jesus wore a crown of thorns; Jesus was pierced. He bore the curse, taking it from us, delivering from the bondage of sin, and from being a prisoner of pride. To anyone who will receive Him, Jesus is able to transform him or her from a thorn into a lily.

His Crown

In *Song 3:11* we see The King crowned on the day of His betrothal. Jesus's crown on the day of His betrothal was a crown of thorns. Thorns again represent the curse, it was with gladness He suffered and bore the curse for us. A crown we know signifies kingship, rulership, and authority; a crown made of thorns placed upon the head of Jesus signified His authority over the curse, both that which produced it, and the consequence.

Remember the Bride is like the Lily; Jesus gave us the key to becoming so, by seeking first the kingdom of God and His righteousness. When we pray with a truthful heart Thy Kingdom come and give us our daily bread, we submit ourselves to God and acknowledge all we have, all sufficiency, is from Him. Though we work to earn the resources necessary to meet our earthly needs, we know the ability to do so is a result of His blessing. We can be free from toil and anxiousness for we know He is our provider, the source of all our ability, all we possess, just as He is the source of our righteousness. He is the source of the grace we need to endure and overcome all the trials and tribulations that are in the world for He has overcome the world. And like Paul we learn to be:

> *Philippians 4:6–7 (KJV)*
> *6 Be careful (anxious) for nothing, but in everything by prayer and supplication with thanksgiving let your requests be made known unto God. 7 And the peace of God, which passeth all understanding, shall keep your hearts and minds through Christ Jesus.*

Are you a Lily or a thorn, are you the model and fragrance of peace and calm or are you fearful, easily pulled to pieces, reactionary, sharp, pointed, piercing, often toxic, or full of toxic emotions, hurtful, and wounding? When the world is falling apart all around you, though it be difficult, and yes there are many things in which this may be naturally impossible, your calm and self-control, evident to all who know and see you, will be a testimony of the peace made only available in Christ. Why? Because like the Lily you have relinquished all control, trusting in God, partaking and receiving of Him, releasing His fragrance, expressing His beauty and grace.

Jesus the Contrasting Fruit

> *Song of Solomon 2:3 (KJV)*
> *3 As the apple tree among the trees of the wood, so is my beloved among the sons. I sat down under his shadow with great delight, and his fruit was sweet to my taste.*

He is the contrasting fruit. Unlike the forbidden fruit Adam and Eve tasted, that which brought curse, death, sorrow, toil, and separation from God; He being the Tree of Life, our partaking of His fruit will nullify these effects, giving life, prosperity, blessing, peace, and so much more. Nurtured, nourished, and protected under the shadow of His covering she now experiences the refuge David spoke of in Psalm 91, and which Ruth obtained through her kinsman redeemer Boaz. No longer alone and unprotected in life she is now under the Kings care and responsibility. Healing likewise in the shadow of His covering wings, she embarks on a journey of restoration and wholeness found only in Him and His word.

She became the Lilly that no longer toils nor spins for the works of her hands now prosper, blessed she now succeeds. She experiences and exhibits the "Fruit of the Spirit"; she has tasted and seen that the Lord is good!

The Banqueting House

He brought me to the banqueting-house, or literally stated, *the house of wine*, as according to the *Brown Driver Briggs Hebrew and English Lexicon*, banqueting is translated wine[3.] It is the place in which believers receive the graces and blessings of Christ. It refers to the place or house where a king or rich vineyard owner would drink the wine. We notice that the King has left the palace and come down into his vineyard seeking out a Bride that was not seeking Him or worthy of Him. Jesus makes clear reference to this in the parable of *The Pearl of Great Price*, also indicating the great price He was to pay, to which Paul also refers in *Romans 10:20*. As we see the Bride invited and brought into the Banqueting-Wine House we come to the offer of betrothal. I sat down in His shade with great delight (under the shadow of His wings) To be brought in we must delight ourselves, desiring nothing on earth more or above the Lord *Song 2:3*.

She says: "He Brought me"; brought is broad in meaning but here it means to lead, guide, or escort a person into, and deeper in meaning it comes from a word meaning to restore. What she is saying in essence is, He is the source, the means, the intermediary, the intervening agency by whose love we are brought through the door into His house, palace, court, and most importantly family. Jesus of course said of Himself I am the good Shepherd and the door, the intermediary by which we enter into restored relationship with God

The Father *(John 10:1–18; 14:6)*. His Banquet, His Table, The Table of the Lord, and wine in Song of Solomon represent communion, intimacy, the place where we come into union with Him, becoming one.

Used as a drink offering, wine symbolizes the suffering of Jesus as He poured out His blood, His total surrender in giving His life as our sacrifice. Paul likewise speaks of being poured out as a drink offering in *2 Timothy 4:6* to symbolize his total surrender even unto death. The point being is one of total surrender, both of Jesus for His Church, and then we in devoting ourselves completely and totally to Him, emptying ourselves which is an act of worship. A worship that must include the root context of the wine house we read of in the Song; it must be enthusiastic, lively, bubbling with emotion and excitement, for it is in fact a celebration a time of rejoicing, the wine *(yayin)* that produces the eyes of the Dove *(Yonah)*, that so captures the heart of the King, the very worship that causes our heart to be one with His *(Song 4:7–9 Psalm 45:10–11)*. (Yonah is thought to be from the same word as yayin meaning effervescent; intoxicating.)

Will you drink from the cup accepting His offer of betrothal? Will you partake of Christ? Will you become intimate with Jesus? Will you come under His Banner?

His Banner over Me Is Love

Banner is a term we all understand as every nation, individual states within nations, individual tribal groups, etc. all including their armies to this day have their defining flags *"banners"* to signify and mark those who are in allegiance with, identity with, and belong to their group. Love is the signifying mark of Jesus and His Bride-Church. We know His love for us was displayed by the price He paid to establish His Church, bring Her into His family, and under His covering and protection. For we who are His Bride, our banner, our mark of identification with Christ is our love for one another *(John 13:34–35)*. But what about our love given to Jesus in return, what does it mean to love Him? Naturally Song of Solomon speaks of affection and love between a man and woman, but let us look further at the definition of love from a Biblical standpoint.

According to *Thayer's Greek Lexicon* the first uses of the Greek term agapé in the Bible are found in the Septuagint (LXX) translation of the Old Testament where ἀγάπη (agapé) is the translation chosen for the Hebrew הָאַהֲבָה (ahabah) in *Song of Solomon 2:4, 5, 7; 3:5, 10; 5:8; 7:6; 8:4, 6, 7. HELPS Word-studies* refers to agápē as love centered on moral preference. So too in secular ancient Greek agápē focuses on preference; likewise the verb form agapáō in antiquity meant, "to prefer" In the New testament agápē typically refers to divine love, which is to say what God prefers. Coming from the cognate agapáō, meaning to prefer, and to love; for the believer it indicates preferring to "live through Christ" *(1 John 4:9, 10)*, embracing God's will, choosing His choices, and obeying them through His power. In essence agapáō refers to Christ living His life through the believer.

Agápē also implies acts of charity, help, or kindness, as a gift! Love in the Hebrew cultural sense refers to how one treats, protects and provides for a privileged gift, such as a spouse, parent, or child. His gift to us is in fact Himself and includes His eternal life in God's presence and so much more we are to inherit with Jesus. And as we have seen, love is a choice; it is to choose someone. So when we read the word love, especially do not stir or awaken love in Song of Solomon we, in one sense, view this as His choosing His Bride, and another His Bride's choice to prefer, to obey, and give her life completely to Him and allow His life to be diffused through her. If we say we love Him but are not sincere in our heart it is meaningless, in fact in Hebraic culture it is a lie if there exist no corresponding action. How we then guard and protect this most valuable of gifts is of utmost importance. This kind of Love is passionate not passive for if it grow lukewarm, if there is no longer obedience, if we do not overcome those "Little Foxes" that corrupt and destroy the relationship, it is no longer acknowledged by Jesus as true love *(Revelation 2:4–5)*.

As stated, banner implies armies and war. The root word banner in *Song 2:4* is from *Exodus 17:15*.

Exodus 17:14–16 (KJV)
14 And the Lord said unto Moses, Write this
for a memorial in a book, and rehearse it in the ears
of Joshua: for I will utterly put out the remembrance
of Amalek from under heaven. 15 And Moses built
an altar, and called the name of it Jehovahnissi: 16
For he said, because the Lord hath sworn that the
Lord will have war with Amalek from generation
to generation.

Moses said: "The-Lord-Is-My-Banner [YHWH Nissi] because He has sworn to have war…"

Notice first though that God said: "I will utterly put (blot) out the remembrance." To blot out the remembrance means to abolish, obliterate from the memory, wipe away, erase, cancel, or remove. It also can mean to touch or smooth with oil. It is through His love, by the anointing of His name and His Spirit that Jesus will totally eradicate the memory and pain of our past and our enemy. This we will examine in more detail in chapter 5.

The identifying mark is love. She is both covered and defended by that which she now identifies; love is her character trait.

Spring: His First Coming

The Purpose of His First Coming

His first coming was to establish covenant, to betroth to Himself a Bride. In *Song 2:9* She says Lo or Behold, He stands behind our wall, He looks through the windows, He gazes trough the lattice. Lo, or Behold is in Hebrew *"hinneh" (hin-nay)*. In our English language behold is to observe a remarkable, impressive person or thing; *hinneh* a word derived from *"hen" (hane)* is to behold as if expressing surprise or astonishment at something unexpected such as an event or fact.

Malachi 3:1 (KJV)
Behold, I will send my messenger, and he shall prepare the way before me: and the Lord, whom ye seek, shall suddenly come to his temple, even the messenger of the covenant, whom ye delight in: behold, he shall come, saith the Lord of hosts.

It appears here that we are instructed to take notice, to be aware of a surprise appearance of a remarkable, impressive person and event. This person and event is God embodied the flesh coming into our realm. She says: He stands; in the Hebrew it is possible to extract a multitude of possibility and inference by this statement such as, He arises, He comes into being, He appears on the scene, and He rises up an army as He dwells, abides, and is stationed behind our wall. Wall here refers to the wall of a house, a dwelling place, yet more importantly the physical body, as we know, is the dwelling place of our soul and spirit. Here the Hebrew word *Kothel* is used. *Kothel* is from a root word meaning to compact, to fit all components into a small space. In one sense what is portrayed here is Jesus, the Word of God, taking on a body made of flesh. In doing so He was able to see and experience completely the nature of man through the eyes and perspective of humanity. For into the windows of our souls He gazed intently with admiration for His lost children, He admitted the light of His truth into the heart and mind of man, affording man the ability to see out of the darkness. Visiting her home, transcending the gap between God and Man, between the supernatural realm of Heaven and the natural realm of earth, our Bridegroom, Jesus, came to betroth to Himself a Bride. Having mediated and enforced this new covenant relationship, in the time of the Jewish Spring Feast.

And yet we must consider her statement, He is looking through our lattice. The crossing of wooden boards is how one made a lattice. I will allow you to contemplate the implications one could derive from that statement alone! Nonetheless, their purpose was to cover windows, patios, or balconies in order to protect, especially women, from the gaze of men. A lattice in essence is a separation device, a hiding mechanism to obscure the view or access. Jesus does not force

His way into our life and soul; He draws us to open ourselves to Him, allowing Him access to our heart and life. Thereby making His Church the interwoven branches connected to and wrapped around Him, the Vine.

Winter Is Past

Song 2:10–13

Winter is past, Spring, the season of the Passover, Firstfruits, and Pentecost, begins the time of new life, a new season, and the outpouring of rain. The season the turtledove, a symbol of the Holy Spirit, appears. It was in this time of year Christ died, rose again, and which Holy Spirit was poured out. Ending the winter season of darkness, death, barrenness, emptiness, unproductiveness, unfruitfulness, and hiding. The curse, death, and darkness, now over and new life, a rebirthing, resurrection, fruitfulness, blessing, and harvest begin. The very time Jesus made all things new.

Ruth, our clearest type or shadow of the Church, as we remember was introduced to, betrothed to, and came under the wing of her redeemer and deliver Boaz at the time of Passover during the barley harvest *(Ruth 2:17)*. Likewise the King's first visit to the Bride's home culminates in the spring of the year as seen in *Song 2:8* through *chapter 3*. It is this critical phase, which we know now was the fulfillment of the feasts of Passover and Pentecost that ushered in the Church Age. As we examine the second half of chapter 2 and much of chapter 3 we see the offer of Betrothal, the Bride price, and the coming of the Holy Spirit. Keep in mind that from Pentecost until the Jewish New Year and the Fall Feasts passes a long, hot, and dry summer season.

In *Song 2:8* we see He comes on the mountains. Prophesied in *Isaiah 52:7* and confirmed by Paul in *Romans 10* Jesus came setting His feet on mountains bringing the good news of salvation first to the Jew then to the Gentile nations. I want to look again at verse 9 of this stanza from a slightly different perspective. Behold, He stands behind our wall, looking through the window and lattice. From His Throne in Heaven Jesus gazed with longing desire for relationship with His creation. He came down from heaven passing through that great gulf between the natural and spiritual realm *(Luke 16:26)*. Traversing and transcending that gap, Jesus came to reconcile and break down the wall of separation between God and Man *(Ephesians 2:14–18)*. As we see in the next verses, calling us out from the winter, the time of death is over, we can enter the spring time of new and restored life. Jesus saying: If you will hear Me, if you will hear the voice of My Holy Spirit, accepting My invitation and the price I have paid for you, I will receive you in the secret place of my presence. And now we must no longer hide from Him. Yes, though His eyes pierce our heart and soul, and Satan attempts to condemn us through a sense of exposure, guilt, shame, or unworthiness, we must not rebuild walls and fences that keep Him at a distance. Nor can we allow fear of losing dignity or control keep us from surrender in worship; we must overcome any fearfulness of His presence. No longer hiding as Adam and Eve afraid because before Him we are naked *(Genesis 3:10)*. No longer should we stand behind walls of vain religious traditions void of real relationship that have a form or appearance of godliness but are nothing more than shadow images of intimacy *(2 Timothy 3:5)*. No, we must surrender to His love and compassion through which He gently draws us into close personal relationship *(Hosea 11:4)*.

Boaz did not take Ruth against her will, no, Ruth we read had to willingly, humbly in surrender approach The Redeemer, The Redeemer who fulfilled all requirements of the Law, a blood relative, willing and able to pay the redemption price. So too must our Bride in Song of Solomon, so too must any who desire to accept the offer made by Christ *(Deuteronomy 25:5–10; John 1:14, 10:7, 15–18; Romans 1:3; Philippians 2:5–8; Hebrews 2:14–15; 1 Peter 1:18–19; Matthew 20:28)*.

The Time of Visitation: The Time to Respond

> *Song of Solomon 2:10–13 (NKJV)*
> *The voice of the King*
> 　　*10 My beloved spoke, and said to me: "Rise up, my love, my fair one, and come away. 11 For lo, the winter is past,*

The rain is over and gone. 12 The flowers
appear on the earth; the time of singing has come,
and the voice of the turtledove is heard in our land.
13 The fig tree puts forth her green figs, and the
vines with the tender grapes give a good smell. Rise
up, my love, my fair one, and come away!

When He calls we must answer. We have been called out of darkness, the principle of sin, and into light, His truth and life. And as *Matthew 22* and *Revelation 19:9* reveal there is a wedding we are called (invited) to attend, many receive the invitation but few accept, few are worthy, and for which few are properly dressed.

In *Song 1:5* she recognized herself as dark like Kedar but lovely, and became one who has said to Him draw "lead" me away. *Gesenius's Hebrew-Chaldee Lexicon* says of Kedar that the word is from Qadar, again meaning dark, dirty, also to mourn or to go in filthy garments as mourners. She is the one that desires conversion, one who accepts Christ. Like the statement in *Hosea 11:4,* He drew her with love; He has healed, fed, and taken off her yoke of oppression, bondage, and subjection (to sin). Excepting His sanctification she has come out from her past dwelling place of darkness, mourning and sorrow. She has exchanged her filthy rags, her unrighteousness for His righteousness seen as she proclaims "like the Tents of Kedar." He draws us not as slaves but sons, not forcing us but giving us the opportunity to voluntarily follow Him, to follow Him out of Kedar and Mesehch *(John 6:35, 44, 12:32; 1 Peter 2:9, Psalm 45:10, 120:5–7, Genesis 12:1–3).*

This is the time to respond to the voice and calling of the Lord, we, as well as the world, must recognize the season. The season in which Holy Spirit has been poured out, the season in which He is speaking and active. The fig tree is in bloom, as *Matthew 24:27–34* counsels, we must recognize the sign of our times, the time is short we do not want to be like those in Jesus day who missed Him, for *Luke 19:41–44* warns of an impending a day when it will be too late for those who knew not their time of visitation, not recognizing the *Kairos* season or opportunity, when God offered it. The offer Jesus makes is for but a limited time, we must make full advantage of that offer while it last. The time to respond is now. *Isaiah 55:6* says seek the Lord while He may be found, which is precisely what we see of the Bride in *Song 3:1–5*. Enter now into covenant for the day will come when the offer is no longer on the table.

The Entering into Covenant

As mentioned, in *Song 2:3* she is seated under His shade or as translated shadow, referring to His protection and shelter. Further study of this word shadow in Hebrew leads to the discovery of the richness of its deeper meaning. *Strong's Exhaustive Concordance* indicates the word to be or from the Hebrew word *tselel*: shadow and coming from *tsalal*: shade, which conveys the idea of hovering over, to overshadow, to sink into rest. In Ruth we see this same idea in the use of the term *under the wing* to describe Ruth's coming under the husband's authority, through a marital covenant whereby Ruth was rescued and entered into a rest so to speak. In Psalms we see under the shadow refers to those who have put their trust in the Lord for protection, those who dwell in His presence, those brought out of darkness, and those delivered from death. The Bride rest in His shadow sheltered and protected having made the choice to come under His authority and to trust in Him (*Ruth 3:9; Psalm 17:8; 36:7–9*). Being delivered from death, being called out of darkness into His marvelous light, we who were once alienated from God have become His, His dwelling place.

Shadows

In *Song 2:17* the Bride makes a reference to the breaking of day, and of the fleeing away of the shadows, along with the Mountains of Bether. *Bether* in Hebrew means "parts" and comes from the word *bather* meaning to cut. Two images we see; one Bether is a depiction of the separation of the Bride and Bridegroom, or in other words, that, which is keeping them apart or separated. And two, the cutting of covenant as found in the use of *bather* describing the separation of an animal in halves as God made covenant with Abraham. Though separated, being overshadowed by the Bridegroom she has entered into covenant relationship. All of which should remind us of another sense of shadow. That is, a shadow as we know, can speak of a copy or representation of a spiritual reality. *Hebrews chapters 8 and 10* point out that the High Priest, Tabernacle, sacrificial offerings, and the Old Covenant were but shadows, mere copies and images, of Christ and our New Covenant in Him. Even so we must not forget the true substance, which they foreshadowed is Christ.

> *Colossians 2:16–17 (NKJV)*
> *16 So let no one judge you in food or in drink, or regarding a festival or a new moon or Sabbaths, 17 which are a shadow of things to come, but the substance is of Christ.*

After the acceptance of betrothal, and covenant has been initiated, the Bride in *Song 4:6* once again refers to the Shadows. Remember just a few stanzas later she remains a garden enclosed a fountain sealed, awaiting the consummation, awaiting that which is soon to come. We too are sealed for the day of redemption, the day He comes for His purchased possession *(Ephesians 1:13–14)*. Though covenanted in relationship, though His Spirit dwells within his Church, we shall remain separated physically as He prepares a home for His Bride.

Job 8:9b…our days on earth are a shadow! A shadow can symbolize that which is not eternal, so she speaks of the day we reach eternity, timelessness, and the end of our mortal lifetime where in we are no longer subject to death.

Until the day breaks, can be translated breaths, or the cool of the day which as we know from the time before Adam fell refers to the time the Lord appears and we stand face to face with Him when the evening or end of the day of separation comes. First mentioned in *Song 2:17* at time of separation (Betrothal) in the word *Bether* we realize she will remain separated, in the place of sanctification until

He returns to redeem His Bride. Lastly, in *Song 4:6* until the "day breaks" she will remain at the mountain of myrrh and hill of frankincense. Till the shadows are gone the Bride will be sustained by His sacrifice.

Shadows also remind us of the prophetic nature of the Song and the Bride. Prophecy can be to forth-tell, to make known the mind, will, or word of God concerning something current, or to foretell, to make known something concerning the future. Prophecy often incorporates demonstrations or signs. God not only speaks through Men and Women, and through His written word, He also demonstrates what is to come through forerunner types and shadows, historical events and persons, one of the most clear-cut examples being Antiochus Epiphanes. The Bride Song of Solomon is a prophetic type or shadow in the same manner that Ruth and Elijah for example are types and shadows of the Church. The Church likewise is, as was John The Baptist, a type and shadow of Elijah who is to come. A restorer of the hearts of the children to the father.

The Dove

Two types of dove are mentioned in Song of Solomon. The first dove mentioned is the same as in the story of Noah in *Genesis 8:8–12*, the other is mentioned in *Genesis 15:9*, where God makes covenant and promises to Abram, and is the same as in the Books of Leviticus and Numbers, the Turtledove, Hebrew *Tor (tore)*, a "clean" morally and ceremonially pure bird acceptable for sacrifice, especially to those poor in estate. Reference to this sacrificial bird is used once in *Song of Solomon 2:12* to refer to a voice heard in the land. The remaining six references to a dove are the Hebrew word *yonah* (yo-naw') a word considered the same as *yayin* (yah'-yin) meaning wine or banqueting wine. The Greek equivalent for *yonah* is used in describing Holy Spirit as He descended as a dove upon Jesus, and Jesus commanded those He sent to be harmless as doves *(John 1:32; Matthew 3:13; 10:16)*.

Soon after she joins herself to His flock, we see the Bridegroom in *Song 1:15* proclaim her to be beautiful, not merely outwardly but inwardly, describing her as having dove's eyes. What is it about the dove that is so important? First it is important to recognize the Turtledove is a symbol of the Holy Spirit *(John 1:32)*, in his book *The Sensitivity of the Spirit* R.T. Kendall explains this concept in great detail.

Secondly, doves are a symbol of innocence, harmless and gentle they express the attributes Jesus desires of His Church *(Matthew 10:16; Philippians 2:14–16)*. As we all are fully aware the Turtledove is a symbol of peace. But what else is there for us to see in the dove? There are many characteristic of the dove important to The Church,

> *The Sensitivity of the Spirit—R.T. Kendal*
> *Kendall says: I have talked with experts on doves and pigeons… They all insist there is virtually no difference between pigeons and doves—unless, however, one is comparing a pigeon to a turtledove…according to Peter Cantrell, the turtle dove is different…* [3]
> *Turtledoves cannot be trained or domesticated… Turtledoves mate with only one partner for Life and never fly farther apart than they can hear each other… Once let out of a cage turtledoves will never return unless there is no other source for food.* [4]

Chaste, faithful, loyal, not conformed to World, not easy to manipulate, control or made to conform, staying close, listening to and for the voice of His Spirit is exactly how Jesus intended His Church to be. Before we speak about the eyes lets look once again at the dove's wings.

The Wings of the Dove

Years ago, the great evangelist Leonard Ravenhill noted that there are nine main feathers on the left and right wings of the dove. He pointed out that there are also nine gifts of the Holy Spirit (1 Cor. 12:7–10) and nine fruits of the Spirit (Gal. 5:22–23). There are also five main tail feathers on a dove, which can represent the fivefold ministry gifts of apostles, prophets, pastors, evangelists and teachers (Eph. 4:11). The tail feathers of a dove are like the rudder of a ship—they assist in balance and direction in flight, just as the fivefold ministry gifts in the church bring balance to the body of Christ.[5] Perry Stone

The Holy Spirit we read in *John 1:32*, descended upon and remained upon Jesus, so too must He with the Bride. A Church functioning without the Holy Spirit and the gifts of the Spirit and without the corresponding fruits or the personality and character traits of Jesus Spirit, one without all five offices of ministry is not a true, healthy, effective Church. We see from the above that the Turtledove requires the nine flying feathers on each wing, the nine gifts of the Spirit and nine fruits of the Spirit, if it is to remain in balance, without them, it cannot not fly. And without the five main tail feathers, ministry offices, the Church has no compass by which it is capable of accomplishing God's will or maintain direction, purpose or truth.

The Eyes of the Dove

Before we speak of the eyes of the Turtledove we need to examine the Hebrew word for this dove, *Yonah,* which as stated, comes from the Hebrew word *yayin* meaning wine in particular a black grape, also meaning a banquet or banqueting. Without jumping back to the banqueting house let's look at the grape and the wine. First of all we know Jesus is the vine and we are the branches upon which the grapes are produced. Not only are we His Church to produce more grapes, by that we mean bring others into the Kingdom and family of God, we are to release the Holy Spirit from within us as rivers of living water. We are to remain connected to and obedient to Him, the Vine if we are to be productive because apart from Jesus we can do nothing *(John 15:1–11)*. Remember She has the eyes of the dove, which should always be focused upon Him. We must keep our eyes on Him alone, faithful, loyal, uncompromising, guarding against the foxes on the prowl that spoil the vine, for we, the tender grapes, are vulnerable, we must guard our hearts, we must protect this relationship not allowing distractions or hindrances to interfere, we must be filled with His Holy Spirit, the Spirit of truth, our comforter, advisor, our protector. Even though our heart remains dedicated it can grow cold, loosing passion, as we will see later things begin to interfere things that undermine and destroy the intimacy. It's little things the enemy often uses to take us away from time with our Lord; the minor distractions that add up until we no longer clearly hear His voice and are no longer responsive to His presence. We must create an environment conducive to the fruitfulness and health of the vine, an environment in which these foxes, which bite and devour, can neither thrive nor survive.

The Voice of the Turtledove

The turtledove is a bird of passage. It appears in Judea early in the spring, when the leaves are coming out, the flowers opening, and every thing looking lovely and beautiful. This will explain some verses in the Song of Solomon, "Rise up, my love, my fair one, and come away, for lo! The winter is past, the rain is over and gone; the flowers appear on the earth; the time of the singing of birds is come, and the voice of the turtle (or turtle-dove) is heard in our land." It remains until summer is gone; and then flies away to a warmer climate to spend the winter. It is in reference to this that David says, "Oh! That I had wings like a dove! For then would I flee away, and be at rest; lo, then would I wander far off, and remain in the wilderness; I would hasten my escape from the windy storm and tempest." You will find these beautiful verses in the Psalm 55.[6] This, I think is very thought-provoking especially when later we will consider The Bride's soul being made as the chariots of her noble people in chapter 6. The voice of the Turtledove is the voice of the Lord and His Spirit calling, drawing those who will to accept Him as their sacrifice, to accept the bride price and offer of betrothal.

Baptism The Mikvah of Living Water

In *Song 4:2 and 6:6* He says like sheep coming up from the washing. Washing here is from the Hebrew word for bathed, washed off or away, the word used for the required ceremonial washing with water for cleansing and consecration of Aaron and his sons before ministering as priest in the presence of God *(Exodus 29:4; 30:20; 40:12)*. The ceremonial washing or Mikvah in a pool of living water is the place where total immersion or as we say Baptism took place. Of the many things the Mikvah symbolizes two are the womb and the grave, hence baptism represents life and death. Baptism through a complete and total immersion signifies sanctification, purification, and transformation, coming under the authority, complete and total devotion, as well as newness of life. It has figurative meanings such as washing, cleansing, initiation, outpouring, fully covered, endued, or to overcome. To be baptized in Christ, as well as baptized with Holy Spirit or endued with His power, is to be covered or clothed in Christ and His Spirit, as we will see in the discussion of the Bride's fragrance. Having put on Christ and His Spirit we are no longer barren, we are made new, we are transformed able to bear *good* fruit even the fruit of the Spirit.

> *Galatians 3:27*
> *27 For as many of you as have been baptized into Christ have put on Christ.*

Having come up out of the water of washing we see purity. Bearing twins, nothing is lacking she is made more than sufficient, obtaining abundantly above all she could ask or think. Her mouth or speech is lovely indicating her heart has been purified for as Jesus said from the heart we speak blessing or cursing, pure or defiled words *(Luke 6:45; Mark 7:14–23; 2 Corinthians 9:8)*.

Two times He mentions her washing. John the Baptist mentions in *Luke 3:16* two types of baptism, water for repentance and the Holy Spirit *(and Fire)*. Other passages mention washing of the Bride, with the water of the word and through the washing of regeneration and renewing of the Holy Spirit *(Ephesians 5:26; Titus 3:5)*. Then again of our bodies and conscience being washed *(Hebrews 10:22)*, and in *1 Corinthians 6:11* that we are washed, sanctified, and justified in the name of the Lord and by Holy Spirit. It is important concerning the doctrine of Baptism and God's divine order to understand, first one believes and accepts Christ as savior, then is baptized in His name followed by the baptism of the Holy Spirit.

The Bride Price

Remember in the Ancient Jewish tradition to enter into betrothal required the payment of the Bride price. Where do we find this concept in scripture? A number of places in fact such as *Genesis 34:12 Exodus 22:16–17,* and *1 Samuel 18:25*, but perhaps our best example is in *Genesis 24* where we read of Abraham seeking to acquire a bride for his son Isaac. This term Bride price or dowry, the Hebrew word *mohar* and its source of origin *mahar* mean the purchase price of a bride, that which is given in exchange for a wife. The payment of and acceptance of the mohar, the gifts given to the bride and typically her father, sealed the betrothal. In the New Testament of course we read the Blood of Jesus is our purchase price *(1 Peter 1:18–19; 1 Corinthians 6:19–20, 7:23; Acts 20:28)*.

But is there any indication of a payment of the Bride price in Song of Solomon? When we look below the surface of the last portion of chapter 3 and on into chapter 4 the answer is yes.

Song of Solomon 3:6–11 (NKJV)
6 Who is this coming out of the wilderness like pillars of smoke, Perfumed with myrrh and frankincense, with all the merchant's fragrant powders? 7 Behold, it is Solomon's couch, with sixty valiant men around it, of the valiant of Israel. 8 They all hold swords, Being expert in war. Every man has his sword on his thigh Because of fear in the night. 9 Of the wood of Lebanon Solomon the King made him-

> *self a palanquin:* **[Chariot or Appiryon]** *10 He made its pillars of silver, its support of gold, its seat of purple, its interior paved with love by the daughters of Jerusalem. 11 Go forth, O daughters of Zion, and see King Solomon with the crown with which his mother crowned him on the day of his espousals, the day of the gladness of his heart.*

The question "Who is this" concerning Jesus can be found a number of times for example *Matthew 21:10 Luke 5:21, 7:49, 9:9,* and *John 12:34.* If you are still not convinced Song of Solomon is a prophetic anticipation of Christ read Matthew or Luke chapter 4. Coming from the wilderness where He overcame and defeated Satan's temptations, all that is in the world, the lust of the flesh, the lust of the eye, the pride of life *(1 John 2:16),* He began His ministry in power and glory. The purpose of His first coming completed on the Cross.

The wilderness can speak of the lost cursed world, the curse that He took upon Himself, as we will see in His crown. Myrrh and Frankincense represent His sacrifice, a sweet smelling aroma to God. War, as we know, Jesus came conquered and disarmed principalities and powers, making a spectacle of them *(Colossians 2:15).*

Perfumed with Frankincense and Myrrh

Frankincense, called pure incense, represents purity. Frankincense is from a root word meaning whiteness and when burned produces a white smoke. Said to be bitter and glittering, it is extracted from the Boswellia serrataas as cuts are made in its bark, the resign dripping out as tears a substance bitter to the taste yet sweet to the smell. The bitterness of the Cross of course making His Church as He, a sweet smelling aroma to God *(Ephesians 5:2; 2 Corinthians 2:14–15).*

Myrrh, meaning bitter in Hebrew, Greek, Latin, and Arabic is a gum resin extracted by cutting gashes the bark of a small desert tree known as the Commifera Myrrha. These cuts or gashes remind us of the wounds and the stripes Christ received while being beaten by the Roman soldiers.

In the Bible Myrrh represent such ideas as:

> Myrrh as a principal ingredient in the holy anointing oil represents anointing, sanctification, setting apart, the dedication and consecration to the Lord (*Exodus 30:23—33*).
>
> Myrrh represents purification, cleansing, and preparation for covenant especially that of intimacy, in particular purification and preparation of a Bride (*Esther 2:12–14*). It was used for the removal of any unpleasant smell *(Sin)* before coming in the presence of the King. It represents being brought up to the standard of royalty (the King).
>
> Myrrh represents sacrificial giving and worship. The Wise Men from the East who came to worship the infant Jesus opened up their treasures giving myrrh as one of their gifts (*Matthew 2:11*).

Myrrh was used in embalming and preparation for burial (*John 19:39*) therefore it expresses death especially dying to self or for another. Bitter to the taste but sweet to the smell, myrrh in the spiritual sense speaks of dying to self to become a *"sweet smelling aroma" to the Lord*.

Myrrh, again bitterness, represents suffering, and sorrow. It was given to those who were condemned to death by crucifixion as an anesthesia to ease the pain and suffering. Jesus was given "wine mingled with myrrh" yet in *Mark 15:23* we read He refused it. And to be discussed later Myrrh is used as medicine for healing.

Jesus, giving Himself for His Bride, is the incense offering, the sweet-smelling sacrifice unto God.

The Bride's Value

Your true value and the understanding of your true value is only recognized by understanding the price He paid for you, which of course was the suffering and death of Jesus. So the question begs, who and what do you allow to determine your value and worth?

Is it your family or friends, society, or the number of friends or followers on your Social Media account? For too many people it is their job, maybe even their ministry, the amount of money they earn, the prestige of their position, the size of crowd they attract or lack thereof. However, for The Church, this is not your true value and these things should never define who we are or what we are worth as a child of God.

If we do not know who we are, who He is, and who we are in Him we will never know the authority we possess or the blessings we possess nor will we know our rights and privileges as Christ's Bride.

The Palanquin (Appiryon)

Chapter 3 verses 6–8 on the surface clearly describe a wedding procession yet prophetically these verses describe the night of Jesus arrest in the Garden, for in verses 9–11 we see His trial, crowning with thorns, and crucifixion. Concealed within the description of His palanquin is His sacrifice; it is the mercy seat, His atonement and propitiation of the Bride.

Song 3:9–10 Solomon the King made himself a Palanquin of:

> *The Wood of Lebanon, which is said to be incorruptible, 1 Peter 1:25 says The Word endures forever,*
> *Silver symbolizing redemption,*
> *Gold symbolizing covered in Glory,*
> *A Purple Seat symbolizing royalty and a throne, and*
> *Love; the inside paved or covered with love.*

In the Palanquin we see salvation and the cost thereof. Occurring only once in scripture, this non-Hebraic word will show Jesus became the vehicle, the means and medium of our salvation. This palanquin, we will discover, portrays the physical body of Jesus!

The wood of Lebanon is considered by most to be from the Cedar Tree. Bear in mind, trees in scripture often refer to men. The Cedar of Lebanon was said to be red in color, bitter to the taste yet fragrant. Red is important in that Adam, the first man or mankind, is from the Hebrew word *Adom* meaning Red! Jesus the second Adam, the Word who became flesh; made Himself flesh, prepared for Himself a body in order to become our sacrifice *(John 1:14; Hebrews 105+)*. Jesus is the Life and the giver of Life; He is the Tree of Life *(John 6:22–58)*, that poured out His blood, again red. Additionally, Cedar is said to be incorruptible, not subject to decay, not consumed by worms, and offensive to insects. The Lord's body of course did not undergo decay or corruption as prophesied in *Psalm 16:10* and confirmed in *Acts 2:31–32*. And as *1 Peter 1:23–25* tells us we are born again through the incorruptible forever enduring Word of God. Made from the cedar of Lebanon this palanquin indicates that which is incorruptible. Jesus the Word who endures forever, in His physical, natural, earthly body was put to death, buried, and resurrected by the power of the Holy Spirit, saw no corruption. Likewise we His Bride will one day inherit incorruption, immortality *(Acts 13:35–37; 1 Corinthians 15:50–55; 1 Peter 1:25)*.

Concerning insects, under the law many were considered unclean. Insects can be destructive, in other words they destroy, and they can carry and transmit sickness and disease. They are food for the birds; in *Revelation 19:17–21* we see the enemies of Christ, those who are deceived by and follow Satan have their flesh eaten by the birds. Insects and worms scripturally can speak of death, plague, and devour. And in *Joel 2* we read God restores what the locust devoured. Our incorruptible Lord, the restorer of our soul, and of our relationship with the Father, defeated the destroyer, and conquered sickness by His bitter suffering and the outpouring of His blood, and most importantly delivered us from death through His resurrection from the grave. The fragrance of His sacrifice, as Paul states in *Ephesians 5:2*, pleasing to God the Father has been transmitted to His Bride *(Song 4:11)*.

In Song 5:15 where it speaks of His countenance being like Lebanon, excellent as the cedars, I suggest that Solomon, under the inspiration of Holy Spirit, alludes to Christ crucified upon the Tree for the cleansing of His Bride. A reference understood when we look back to *Leviticus 14:4, 6, 49, 51, and 52* and see cedar was instrumental in ritual cleansing and purification.

> *Song of Solomon 3:10 (KJV)*
> *10 He made the pillars thereof of silver, the bottom thereof of gold, the covering of it of purple, the midst thereof being paved with love,...*

The Palanquin in *Song of Solomon 3* also called the Appiryon (ap-pir-yone'), Litter, or Bridal Carriage is a portable enclosed chair for one person, normally royalty or a Bride, it brings to mind the Tabernacle, in particular the Ark of the Covenant. Like the Ark it consisted of poles that enabled it to be carried. Litter is an old word for a stretcher used to carry a sick or wounded person. Solomon may not have intended this but God knowing the future Latin based languages may have for as Isaiah prophesied:

> *Isaiah 53:4 (KJV)*
> *4 Surely he hath borne our griefs, and carried our sorrows: yet we did esteem him stricken, smitten of God, and afflicted.*

This wedding carriage describes marriage both of the Corporate Church and the individual Bride or Believer. It is descriptive of Jesus the wounded King, Jesus of course as prophesied wounded for our salvation in the house of His friends *(Isaiah 53:5; Zechariah 13:6)*. Jesus in whom is the healing for a wounded humanity.

In the description of this chariot within which the bride is carried to her bridegroom we begin to see the mohar. This chariot, depicting the covenant of redemption, forgiveness, and salvation, made of:

> Pillars of SILVER
> Silver, upright, that which make His Bride upright is the framework of silver speaking of

course of redemption, the price of the soul, and deliverance from bondage, slavery, and oppression ours of course being the blood of Jesus *(Leviticus 5:15; Exodus 30:11–16; Matthew 27:3–9; 1 Peter 1:18–20; Ps. 105:37)*.

Support or the foundation GOLD

Gold represents His glory, grace, and kingship, and our coming into His Kingdom, under His authority *(Job 37:22; Revelation 3:18, 4:4, 14:14; Matthew 2:11; Psalm 45:9, 13)*. We trust not in the gold itself nor do we honor it for even Peter writes our faith is more precious than gold however, we must understand what it can represent *(1 Peter 1:7)*. Gold is that which is precious and pure. Gold is representative of Jesus Himself as well as His Church *(Revelation 1:20)*. In *Song 5:11* The King's head is of this gold! The Hebrew word used is *kethem (keh'-them)* meaning fine gold or pure gold. Thus it represents the highest and purest quality, highest value. Used also in *Psalm 45:9* the Bride of the King standing at His Right Hand is arrayed in this gold! Remember the right hand represents authority as she reflects the light of His glory she likewise represents His authority. The Bride in our Song has a neck of gold and is given ornaments of gold. What is even more interesting is that *Kethem* is from the word *katham (kaw-tham')* meaning to be stained, blood stained, marked, and to cover or conceal, both reflect the idea of engraving. Does the passage in Isaiah *inscribed on the palm of My hands* of ring a bell? Concerning stained,

Isaiah 1:18 (KJV)

18 Come now, and let us reason together, saith the Lord: though your sins be as scarlet, they shall be as white as snow; though they be red like crimson, they shall be as wool.

Revelation 19:13–15 (KJV) see also Isaiah 62:2–3
13 And he was clothed with a vesture dipped in blood: and his name is called The Word of God.

14 And the armies which were in heaven followed him upon white horses, clothed in fine linen, white and clean.

15 And out of his mouth goeth a sharp sword, that with it he should smite the nations: and he shall rule them with a rod of iron: and he treadeth the winepress of the fierceness and wrath of Almighty God.

Seat of PURPLE
Song of Solomon 7:5 (KJV)
…and the hair of thine head like purple…

The Palanquin's seat (Authority) is of purple. Purple is a composite of blue and red. Red speaks of Christ's body and blood; purple scripturally speaks of royalty, a King, and therefore, authority. Purple was placed on Jesus in a mocking insult because He claimed to be a King. A woman's hair speaks of her covering her submission to authority. The Brides hair being purple denotes the King both covers her and is the authority over her.

Mention is made in the Old Testament of two kinds of purple, or purple dye: (1) "argaman" (Aramaic, "argevan" Greek, π ό ρ φ υ ρ α), probably the bright-red purple, which was costliest when it had the color of coagulated blood, and appeared black when viewed directly, but lustrous red when viewed obliquely (2) "tekelet" (Greek, ὑ ά κ ι ν 9 ο ς), which, according to Philo and Josephus, resembled the color of the sea, the air, or the clear sky, and was, therefore, termed also blue. In instances it was black or dark-colored.[7] The 1901 Jewish Encyclopedia

Purple represents His throne, His royalty, and the His Bride as a royal priesthood seated in Heavenly places with Christ *(1 Peter 2:9; John 19:1–5; Ephesians 1:20)*.

The seat, or chariot as Solomon chose to call the covering of the Ark of the Covenant is the Mercy Seat, which translates Propitiation.

> *1 Chronicles 28:18 (KJV)*
> *And for the altar of incense refined gold by weight; and gold for the pattern of the chariot (Mercy Seat Exodus 25:17–22) of the cherubims, that spread out their wings, and covered the ark of the covenant of the Lord.*

> *Romans 3:24–25*
> *24 Being justified freely by his grace through the redemption that is in Christ Jesus: 25 Whom God hath set forth to be a propitiation through faith in his blood, to declare his righteousness for the remission of sins that are past, through the forbearance of God;*

Just as the mercy seat of pure gold covered the law of sin and death, and the curse, Jesus, who out of an indescribable love for mankind became our propitiation *(1 John 2:2, 4:10)*, has atoned and covered by substitution our guilt, and sin, and has appeased the wrath of God. Now blessed, reconciled, and restored to God's family we are fully able to enter and abide in God's presence.

The seat paved, or fit together, inlaid and covered with LOVE. What about cover? Our sin and lawless deeds are covered (concealed), and we know love covers sin *(Romans 4:7; 1 Peter 4:8)*. The blood of Jesus of course covered our sin as He demonstrated the greatest act of love known to mankind by giving His life to purchase our salvation and everlasting life.

Two things I want to consider about this love; first betrothal, our redemption and salvation, cannot be earned or purchased by our own righteousness or religious efforts no matter how valuable, worthy, or honorable we may deem them. Though we bear fruits of righteousness to think we can earn redemption by works or religious ritual is an insult to His blood. This gift which we have obtained cannot be bought, worked for, or transferred. Second if we look from Jesus's point of view, tragically and to His deepest sorrow the price He paid is by many despised and rejected.

Fashioned by the King is a chariot with which to take His Bride away one that she alone must make the decision to enter, for there is no other way to salvation, everlasting life, or The Father except through Him, Jesus. She must be carried in Him for, no works; nothing in her power or efforts, no price she can pay can accomplish this deliverance, redemption, and relationship.

As chapter 3 concludes we see the King wearing the CROWN given to Him on the day of His betrothal, His Crown on the day of His betrothal was a crown of thorns. Thorns as we know represent the curse, which He took upon Himself as He hung on the tree exchanging Himself for His Bride accepting it on her behalf, setting her free from the dominion and curse of sin.

As we read in chapter 4 she has accepted this offer to enter into relationship. Now He defines and describes her as pure and clean, blessed, fruitful, and prosperous. Having come out of the world (verses 7–9) she is spotless. Having captivated and received His heart, she begins to become a reflection of His glory, and, as we will see later, emitting His very fragrance.

Once more, we should never lose sight of the fact that the Bride had to agree to the price and accept the gifts for the betrothal to be in effect. The gifts signifying love, commitment, and loyalty Christ gave to His Church as He ascended to Heaven include the gift He promised of the Holy Spirit *(Acts 2:38, 10:45; Ephesians 4:7–8)*. I feel it necessary to say something more concerning the gifts. Note the detail in *Genesis 24* of Abraham sending gifts to Rebecca, Isaac's potential bride. First we notice Abraham sent his servant whom we realize to be named Eleazar from *Genesis 15:2*. Eleazar, *EL*—God, and *EZER*—my helper, means God is my help; remember the Holy Spirit is called the helper in *John 14:26*. Note in *Genesis 24:10* that this servant took 10 camels one camel was for the bride to ride and the other nine were full of gifts for the bride. As Derek Prince once said, accepting the gifts meant her commitment of herself as a bride to Isaac, in this she honored Isaac. Rebekah's refusal to accept the gifts would have meant rejection of Isaac, a dishonor of him.

Our gift or one of our gifts we should say is the Holy Spirit who as we know comes with nine primary gifts for the Church to receive *(1 Corinthians 12:7–10)*. And the Bride is clearly defined in *John 13:20* as those who receive the Holy Spirit, for those who receive Jesus will also receive Him whom Jesus sends. Those who have genuinely received and belong to Jesus receive, accept, and are possessed by the Holy Spirit. Just as Rebecca accepted the master's gifts brought by the servant of the master and was willing to go with or follow the master's servant, so too must we as Jesus Bride accept and follow the Holy Spirit.

Today God has sent as our guarantee, as proof that He will one day fulfill His promise to return for His Bride, our future redemption and eternal life in His presence, His Holy Spirit with Gifts for the Bride. And by accepting these gifts we designate ourselves as a committed bride of Jesus.

> *Ephesians 1:13–14 (KJV)*
> *13 In whom ye also trusted, after that ye heard the word of truth, the gospel of your salvation: in whom also after that ye believed, ye were sealed with that holy Spirit of promise, 14 Which is the earnest of our inheritance until the redemption of the purchased possession, unto the praise of his glory.*

A final note concerning the palanquin, as the palanquin was carried by men, so too is the message of the Cross of Christ ours to carry, as we like Paul, take up our cross daily. Regarding the sixty men surrounding the Palanquin, many theories, I would venture to guess, have been proposed but what I found most interesting is the Hebrew word for sixty, transliterated *shishshim*. *Brown-Driver-Briggs Hebrew-English Lexicon* points out that *shishshim* is an indeclinable noun having only one form, having no inflections, no affixation, no derivation, no separate illustration. Therefore it is a set form allowing no modification, unalterable, non-changeable. And so is the work of Jesus on the cross, so too is our salvation.

Chapters 2 and 3 describe the individual acceptance of His first coming and how Jesus paid the Bride Price. He came to seek and save the lost *(Luke 19:10)* but we must, as Jesus said, come to Him; we must seek Him *(Mark 8:34–38)*. Those who genuinely come to Him will bring Him into every area of their life *(Song 3:4)*.

Kallah: The Perfect and Complete Bride

The Hebrew Word for Bride again is kallah: which is from Kalal meaning perfected, or completed. But how is this made possible? First of course is seen in *John 19:30*.

> *John 19:30*
> *30 When Jesus therefore had received the vinegar, he said, It is finished: and he bowed his head, and gave up the ghost.*

Helps Word Studies states that finished is the Greek word transliterated *teleó* meaning to bring to an end, to complete, to fulfill. *Teléō* is from *télos*, meaning consummation, completion, or to finish the necessary process with the results of rolling-over to the next level or phase of consummation. *Strong's Concordance* says *télos* includes the idea of to discharge, pay for, or make an end of a debt. So what we see here is the Bride price has been paid in full. And as a result, the Bride has been made perfect a fact seen in the very definition of Bride, *Kallah (kal-law')* from *Kalah (kaw-lal')* meaning perfected, completed, or made perfect. Having been made perfect by the Bride Price Jesus paid on the Cross; the Bride by definition possesses all the required qualities, characteristics, made free from flaw, defect, or imperfection she now satisfies the necessary conditions and requirements of a Bride fit for the King. She is made complete, made whole or perfect, appropriate. For as Jesus through Solomon prophesied over the Bride:

Song of Solomon 4:7 (KJV)
        7 Thou art all fair, my love; there is no spot in thee.

And in Song of *Solomon 5:2 and 6:6*, He says she is His perfect one, complete, undefiled, blameless, guiltless having no spot, blemish, defect, and no moral stain.

Hebrew nouns and verbs are derived from roots, roots tell us the essence of the word, the true substance. The individual and unalterable nature if you will. So the Spouse or Bride is the forever perfected and completed one, hence the reason He calls her My perfect one. The question is how does she, how do we become the perfect one? The answer is accepting the price He paid and His offer of redemption.

He has perfected every area, every issue in her life both real and imagined, the things she thought were flaws or imperfections, taking care of her tendency toward perfectionism if you will! He has thus restored her soul, her mind, reasoning and thoughts, her will, and her emotions. She is complete in Him, completed by Him. He has, or can fill every empty void in her soul. As *Hebrews 10:14* indicates: Jesus perfected forever those being sanctified, and as *Colossians 2:10* tells us, we are Complete in Christ. And so the Father sees the Church in Christ as the image and reflection Jesus, restored to His likeness made perfect and complete. As *Acts 17:28* says: In Him we live in move, have our being. Again the question was: How is this accomplished? We see the course of action in her statement in chapter 2.

He Is Mine, I Am His

Song of Solomon 2:16a (KJV)
        16 My beloved is mine, and I am his.

Notice in Song 2:16 the Bride says: "My beloved is mine and I am His"

The Order is critical

1. He is mine

Then

2. I belong to Him

She must first accept Him, making Him her Lord before she belongs to Him and in this decision the process of perfection takes place. The Hebrews roughly reads My Beloved, "*my loved one, my betrothed*" is to, and I to "*Him.*" We are then, *to* one another, so what is it in this word to we need to understand, what might "to" mean? To, identifies the recipient of something. To, identifies the relationship between one person and another. To, identifies two things attached. And *to* pinpoints the person or thing affected. To be affected is to be acted upon or influenced in order to produce an effect or change in. To be effected is to be changed as a result of, or by consequence of an action. We are called to be His. If you are His, "to Him" you cannot be "to" anyone or anything else.[3]

All that is yours becomes or is given to Him, and all that is His becomes, or is given to you. Sin, worry, fear, insecurity, offense, sickness, wounds, pains, suffering, depression, bondage, whatever the case may be you give to Him in exchange for His life, righteousness, healing, peace, liberty, joy…

Yet we must bear in mind, man and wife are one when they give themselves to one another. It is a choice; it is a decision. Any part or anything, any area that we do not give is an area closed off, one that we retain, any area in which we cannot or do not receive that which is His, cannot change. It becomes or is in fact an area where by we limit God by not allowing Him access.

Scripture reference:

Galatians 2:20 (KJV)

20 I am crucified with Christ: nevertheless I live; yet not I, but Christ liveth in me: and the life which I now live in the flesh I live by the faith of the Son of God, who loved me, and gave himself for me.

Romans 14:7–8
7 For none of us liveth to himself, and no man dieth to himself. 8 For whether we live, we live unto the Lord; and whether we die, we die unto the Lord: whether we live therefore, or die, we are the Lord's.

Concerning marriage, as Paul explains in *1 Corinthians 7:32–34*, our goal is not to live self-serving, self-seeking, self-pleasing, self-willed lives but rather live to please the Lord. And no matter the outcome of events we belong to Him.

Note: Sanctification does involve decisions, actions, behaviors on our part but salvation, with the exception of ones decision to accept it, does not, for if salvation is in anyway based upon what we do, who we are, then it is of ourselves not Jesus, who is the only source of salvation!

CHAPTER 3
Sanctification and His Return to His Father's House

As stated Song of Solomon is layered in meaning, point being within a passage more than one message can be illustrated. I believe chapter 3 of Song of Solomon depicts more than a wedding procession. It speaks of sanctification, the Bride being called out of slumber, and her being drawn into deeper levels of intimacy beyond that of institutionalized religion. Hidden even deeper, I believe, is reference to the death, burial and resurrection of Christ, the birth of the Church in Jerusalem, and the beginning witness or spread of the Gospel.

My question is; whom does a person search for at night from bed? One can only in the soul; in ones mind and thoughts search from this position. Jesus, speaking of His death in *John 9:4*, told His disciples He must do the that which the Father sent Him to do while it was day, for the night was coming in which no man can work. As He was in the grave night came upon the world, as Jesus was cut off from the world, and the Disciples were cut off from His presence, that which Isaiah and Daniel prophesied was fulfilled *(Isaiah 53:8 Daniel 9:26)*. But on the third day certain women rose up to visit His tomb, by these and others He was found to be alive. Having appeared to His followers numerous times over the following forty days, taken up into heaven before their eyes, filling them with His Spirit on the day of Pentecost, the Church was birthed in Jerusalem. Chapter 3 portrays the followers of Christ coming out of hiding to begin their witness, the spread of the gospel, the message of His death, burial, and resurrection, that which we have spoken of in chapter 2 in the description of the palanquin.

I Could Not Find Him

As Song of Solomon chapter 2 ends and chapter 3 begins we see the Betrothal period in particular through the use of the word Bether, or translated "mountain of separation"

> *Song of Solomon 3:1–4 (KJV)*
> *3 By night on my bed I sought him whom my soul loveth: I sought him, but I found him not.*
> *2 I will rise now, and go about the city in the streets, and in **the broad ways** I will seek him whom my soul loveth: I sought him, **but I found him not**.*
> *3 The watchmen that go about the city found me: to whom I said, Saw ye him whom my soul loveth?*
> *4 It was but a little that I passed from them, but I found him whom my soul loveth: I held him, and would not let him go, until I had brought him into my mother's house, and into the chamber of her that conceived me.*

In verse 2 of chapter 3 is one of many profound statements in the Song that begs discussion. Repeated in chapter 5 after the Bridegroom comes knocking on the door of her heart, it is one that you may find challenging, some may even consider it offensive; it is not meant to be condemning, nevertheless comment must be made. Solomon speaks of the Bride seeking the Bridegroom in the broad way or squares using the word *"rechob."* This word can and of course does refer to the town square but more importantly, when we consider the verb *"rachab"* from which it comes it refers to the enlarged or wide places. Again, remember in these passages she is speaking of seeking the Bridegroom, who as previously stated is Jesus. She does not find Him in the broad or *wide* places; for as Jesus said in *Matthew 7:13–14* narrow is the way to life, the wide or broad way leads to destruction, eternal separation.

Notice, she need go beyond the watchmen in order to find Him. Watchmen are those on the inside, they refer to religious leaders, institutionalized religion, those who are called and charged with being ministers of Christ, rulers of the Church charged with keeping, protecting, preserving, and guarding the faith. Evidently those she encounters are like many today who have become nothing more than guardians of ceremonial ritual, denominational doctrine, religious traditions, and especially those who have, as Paul said would transpire, fallen away into apostasy. Many of whom, just as the religious leaders of Jesus's day, have no idea who Jesus really is, nor do they desire Him, such cannot help you "find" the one for whom you are passionate. Religious rituals, traditions, and incantations are hollow substitutes, empty, void, and unable to provide any actual experience of true intimate relationship with Jesus. As Jesus said of the religious leaders of His day in *Matthew 23:13*, they neither enter into the Kingdom of God nor do they allow others to do so. Remember if Jesus was rejected and despised by such so too will His true Bride be today.

Time of Separation: The Sanctified Bride

Sanctification is expressed throughout Song of Solomon; in particular chapter 2 verses 10, 13, 17 and chapter 4 verse 6–8. What we find in deeper study of these passages and others is that sanctification, beginning with salvation, is our Christian walk. It is not a mere a one-time event, but a continual life long process. As we read in *1 Thessalonians 2:13; 4:1–12 chapter 5* and particularly *5:23*, before the coming of the Bridegroom for we who are His Bride, we are to remain sanctified, we are to be an example to the world, we are to watch and be sober. A concept Solomon describes using terms such as: Bether, come away, and come down as he illustrates the drawings and leading of the Bride by the Bridegroom.

Sanctification or holiness, expresses possession and ownership. It is our surrendering of our will and the rights to our life to the Lord. Though often easier said then done, it is a continual process of growth and maturity in one's relationship with Christ. One made possible not by will power alone, but by the empowerment of the Holy Spirit. The sign of the degree to which we have sanctified ourselves is the measure of God's presence and His grace both in us and with us, *See Exodus 33:15–16.* And the more we separate from the world's behaviors, opinions, and attitudes, the more like Jesus we become. In this time of separation we should be growing in the character and nature of Christ. By the power of Holy Spirit, and the renewing of our minds as the Apostle Paul said, from one level of glory to the next level of glory we are being conformed into the image of Christ *(2 Corinthians 3:18; Romans 12:1).* As our thoughts and attitudes are conformed to those of Christ, so too will our character, will, and desires change until more and more we began to think and act like Jesus. Even as those in the early church who acted so much like Christ they were mockingly labeled "Christians."

> ***SANCTIFICATION*** *International Standard Bible Encyclopedia*
>
> *For those who are in Christ are a new creation (2 Corinthians 5:17), and those to whom has come the separating and consecrating call (2 Corinthians 6:17) must cleanse themselves from all filthiness of the flesh and spirit, perfecting holiness in the fear of God (2 Corinthians 7:1). Paul looks upon the members of the church, just as he looks upon the church itself, with a prophetic eye; he sees them not as they are, but as they are to be. And in his view it is "by the washing of water with the word," in other words by the progressive sanctification of its members, that the church itself is to be sanctified and cleansed, until Christ can present it to Himself*

a glorious church, not having spot or wrinkle or any such thing (Ephesians 5:26, Ephesians 5:27)[1].

The Drawings or Leadings of the Bridegroom

Song of Solomon 2:10, 13 (KJV)
10 My beloved spake, and said unto me, Rise up, my love, my fair one, and come away... Arise, my love, my fair one, and come away

In Hebrew it reads something like: Rise up to Me and come away. Rise up, the Hebrew word *qum,* means to abide or to rise up to the place of abode, to remain, to be upheld (supported, sustained, maintained), and in a military sense to take your stance or position. Come away, the Hebrew word *halak,* means to accompany, walk, access, become, approach, follow, continue (with), or grow.

Many today are being either called out from or called to awaken from within traditional religious institutions and denominations. God is calling and leading many out of complacency, out of man-made doctrines and practices of abstract intellectualized religion back to concrete experiential relationship with Jesus. Though the Apostasy, the falling away, is taking place across much of the so-called Church, Jesus still has those whose hearts are truly devoted to Him that He is drawing deeper. There is no margin for complacency or apostasy if you are the Bride. Jesus, as we see in the Song of Solomon example, is continually calling, pursuing, and compelling His Bride to a new and deeper level of relationship, to always move forward and grow, to never become stagnant in her walk, never satisfied with yesterdays encounter.

The fist calling, we saw previously, is the call to salvation through His redemption; it is our being "Drawn out of Darkness."

Song of Solomon 1:4–5
4 Draw me away! We will run after you... I am dark but lovely...like the tents of Kedar... The king has brought me into his chambers.

Notice the word *draw*, we see it also in *John 6:44* where Jesus proclaims that no one can come to Him unless the Father draws that person, which as we know is an open invitation to any who so desire to be drawn, for Jesus also said in *John 12:32* when Crucified, He will draw all peoples to Himself.

The cry of the Bride is and must be: draw me, compel me, persuade me, convenience and encourage me to follow after You, to come into the dwelling place of Your presence. As we recognize His leading we must follow in pursuit of His salvation, peace and, presence.

The first call or drawing, the salvation call, then is to intimate relationship; it is the offer to abide in Christ. As with the Bride in *Song of Solomon 1:5–13*, we are called out of darkness and sanctified as a member of His flock. Not only does the Bride allow Him into her heart, she is likewise brought into His. As we read in chapter 2 she is a lily among thorns in the valley, a Bride brought out of and redeemed from the curse of sin. She, like Ruth, is delivered from the depths of hopelessness to reside under the shadow of her Redeemer's wings. She has been awakened under the apple tree and partaken of His fruit, His life *(see Song 2:3, 8:5)*, made a part of His vineyard, upheld, sustained, and now covered by His love and compassion.

Regarding salvation, we are given a description of the time of Jesus first coming in *Song 2:10–14*, Winter has passed the time of singing "rejoicing" has come, the voice of the Turtledove is heard; now is her time to rise up and come away. This of course speaks of the season of Passover to Pentecost, God's appointed time for Jesus to be crucified for our redemption and for the coming of the Holy Spirit. The very drawing of all peoples to Himself Jesus spoke of in *John 12:32*. This passage speaks of a new day, new life, a new season, harvest, and fruitfulness. It speaks of His pierced side, and for those who accept His offer it describes our being hidden in Christ, our Rock; as David spoke of *Psalm 91*, it speaks of hiding our life in the secret place of His presence.

As Time Goes by Euphoria Turns to Familiarity

Most of us can relate our own salvation experience and the closeness we felt to Jesus in the beginning with that of the Bride in our Song. In many of our lives, just as with our Bride example in *Song 2:15–3:4,* foxes eventually creep in, distractions begin to hinder the relationship; as with the Bride, our passion starts to cool. Suddenly we find ourselves separated *(Bether)* with a lost sense of His presence. Sadly, at this juncture many who accept Christ simply fade away not realizing that they, just as with the Bride in the Song, are being drawn into deeper intimacy and maturity by a sense of the absence of His presence. It is in chapter 3 verses 1 through 4 that we find the proper response; we must be, as this Bride at this time, quick to make the necessary adjustments in our lives. Separated, weary perhaps; even falling asleep, she nonetheless senses of His tug upon her heart. It is through the lost sense of His presence that Jesus actually calls out to His Church. When she no longer senses His presence, the Bride must awaken and seek Him with all her heart and soul. In doing so she realizes the level of relationship He desires to have with her is not found the old man-made ways and traditions. No, they have become veils or walls of separation. She must come out from behind the lattice if she is to grow *(Song 2:9).*

Watchmen

As we said she encounters the Watchmen in chapters 3 and 5; Watchmen again are persons on the inside, guardians of the City, of the traditions and doctrines of the "Church." Allow me to qualify this by stating: of course we need teachers and leaders in the Body of Christ to ensure we maintain valid doctrinal truths and practices. This is not meant to suggest otherwise. Yet in the manner Solomon speaks of them in the Song, they are religious leaders with no interest in a submitted, intimate relationship with Christ, nor do they desire any true encounter with Jesus. Those Solomon portrays are those who will defend their man-made doctrines, rituals, and traditions at the expense of a personal, experiential relationship with Jesus. Those

Solomon presents to the reader in his Song are ones having no idea where Jesus is, they have become of no help in finding Him. And in chapter 5 just as Jesus forewarned His disciples, they even persecute and excommunication those who passionately seek Him sincerely believing it is their sacred duty to God to do so *(John 16:2–3)*. She must pass them by if she is to experience His presence once again.

Further understanding as to who the Watchmen are will require looking back to the time of Christ and examine the idea of Watchmen through the Pharisees, the Sadducees, the Sanhedrin, and the Synagogue. Watchmen historically speak of the Jewish Priests, spiritual ministers, including blind or false teachers *(Isaiah 62:6; Hebrews 13:17; Isaiah 56:10)*. Those who prefer traditions to truth just as those who hated the Messiah, those who should have recognized Him from the scriptures and His fulfillment of the prophecies, those who loved their prominence and traditions so much so that those very traditions blinded them *(Matthew 15:14)* even to the point of accusing Him as being of the Devil, does this sound familiar?

Pharisees "separated" sanctimonious, ritualistic, legalistic, traditionalist, often hypocritical, who rigidly upheld the traditions of man and emphasized the ceremonial and outward appearance rather than relationship. Their interpretation of the Law of Moses *"Scripture"* was more important and authoritative than the actual Law *"Scripture"* itself. These Jesus said are blinded to the truth, to Jesus and Holy Spirit. They are those who do not, and who hinder others from experiencing the manifestation of the Kingdom of Heaven influencing and impacting their lives *(see Matthew 23:13; Luke 11:52; John 3:1–12)*. Pharisees not only attempted to bait Jesus into making heretical statements they also falsely accused Him of doing so. And so will this type of person do today.

Sadducees, represent those who compromise with society, the Zeitgeist if you will, to maintain status and reputation. This group comprised of Priest, businessmen, and the wealthy, were the elite, and intellectual of Jewish society who compromised with Rome to gain privilege.

Sanhedrin, "Council" the court, headed by the High Priest was the ruling body among the Jews comprised of Scribes, Pharisees, business leaders and the wealthy. Today they might be called the committee, the Board, or the Association for example. This group held considerable influence on religious matters. Their influence not only would have exerted control in Jewish society but in the Synagogues as well. Yet again, as I stated I do not suggest that all Associations, Boards, or Committees are to be considered a hindering "watchmen," some are of great value. Remember, we all need and must be held accountable to authority.

The Synagogue, the congregation, is the model for and represents our modern day local church or denominational group. Lead by a local Rabbi these institutions dominated the religious thinking and opinions of the day. Today there are good, healthy, spirit led congregations as well as misguided and false doctrinal institutions. For this reason we need, as Paul also spoke of, the gift of discerning of spirits.

All of these can be found in *The Church* today and can include Christian leaders, various churches and their denominations, Christian media, and of course individuals. However, before judging just who a Watchman might be, we must judge ourselves as to if, and when at times, we are one of the so-called Watchmen! And more importantly, we must consider the principles of authority and spiritual authority. God who ordained authority also requires us to honor and respect those in authority. Therefore, caution must be taken before, or if ever, we judge or accuse anyone of being such a "Watchman," yet we must also be aware of the widespread existence of such in the so-called Christian community. However, prudence demands we remember the saying: "that which you compromise to gain you will ultimately lose." As with those in Jesus's day who compromised to gain and maintain lost it all, so too will we if we compromise with the world today.

Sanctification: Taking Up Your Cross

In *Song 4:6–8* we see once again the Bride drawn to an even deeper level of sanctification and relationship, cautioned against complacency and empty ritual, and instructed to discern the apostate. In *Song 4:6* in particular through the use of the word Bether, or translated "mountain of separation" which represents self sacrifice, self denial, and the bitterness of death to self and one's own will, plan, purpose, and the word Frankincense, representing prayer and worship, we see sanctification as her decision to die daily.

The Bridegroom says *come from*: meaning to look, to take notice, study, contemplate, or consider. He is instructing the Bride that she needs be aware of some things and concerns as revealed in the terms used. Jesus, through these word illustrations, summons His Church to the place of discernment, where she can see and understand clearly.

Come from Lebanon, Lebanon has many positive illustrations even in other references in the Song, but in this case the Bridegroom summons the Bride from pride and her comfort zone *(See Jeremiah 18:14; Isaiah 2:13; 2 Kings 14:9–10; Hosea 14:7; Ezekiel 31:16)*. For what we see later in chapter 5 she is called to the harvest fields, to evangelize in the heat of battle.

Look from the summit of Amana, Amana comes from a word meaning faith, agreement, and covenant. It refers to that which is fixed, certain, sure, a firmly established regulation. In *The Passion Translation* of the Bible Dr. Brian Simmons notes Amana can refer to the place of settled security. It appears then He is calling His Bride from complacency, from satisfaction with the status quo. Look from the summit of Senir and Hermon, Senir, which is simply another name for Hermon, is a sacred mountain in Syria and Northern Israel. Hermon is from a word meaning sacred, devoted to religious uses, forfeited, or accursed in that is has been dedicated to or for religious practices. Is it yet clear that Jesus repeatedly calls us away from the pride, trust, and a place of satisfaction and security in vain, if not idolatrous, religious ceremony and ritual back to personal relationship?

When He says came from the lion's dens and the mountain of leopards He is instructing His Bride to discern the spirits, in particular that of apostasy. We have all seen documentaries of lions and leopards, predators, tenacious defenders of their territory. The leopard being spotted, speaks of that which is stained, or tainted and often refers to that which is corrupt, defiled, or impure. In *Jeremiah 13:23* the leopard represents the unchangeableness of moral character in those who prefer to do evil instead of good. Leopards are camouflaged, opportunistic hunters in the night that adapt to various environments. Able to disguise themselves, these are, as Jesus referred, wolves in sheep's clothing, those who take advantage of the darkness, preying upon ignorance or weakness of others.[2] Lions, like the leopards also maintain guarded territorial boundaries they however dwell in close-knit social groups. Lions speak of strength, royalty, kings, those possessing authority, and power. Jesus, as we know, is referred to as the Lion of the tribe of Judah. But we must remember lions in scripture can refer to ungodly rulership, strength, and power as well.

> *1 Peter 5:8 (KJV)*
> *8 Be sober, be vigilant; because your adversary the devil, as a roaring lion, walketh about, seeking whom he may devour:*

> *Revelation 13:2 (KJV)*
> *2 And the beast which I saw was like unto a leopard, and his feet were as the feet of a bear, and his mouth as the mouth of a lion: and the dragon gave him his power, and his seat, and great authority.*

> *Jeremiah 5:6 (KJV)*
> *6 Wherefore a lion out of the forest shall slay them, and a wolf of the evenings shall spoil them, a leopard shall watch over their cities: every one that goeth out thence shall be torn in pieces: because their transgressions are many, and their backslidings are increased.*

Revealed in the deeper study of the words Solomon uses in verse 8, Jesus is summoning His Bride to depart from vain religious practices, from mere social gatherings, from contentment with the status quo, from worldliness, and apostasy. What Holy Spirit seems to have used Solomon to do is give the Bride an encrypted warning, one corresponding to the words of the Apostles Peter, Paul, and Jude, to separate herself from the complacency and the apostasy of false teachers, from pretentious spiritual leaders and their doctrine, *(2 Peter 2–3; 2 Thessalonians 2; Jude)*.

Called out of Slumber

In chapter 4 the Bride is being called out of the vanity of systematic religion and apostasy back to relationship. In chapter 5 the Bride is drawn out of sleep, lethargy, indifference, and self-righteousness. The focus is one of Revival and Awakening. He comes to awaken her, to rekindle her passion. Notice once again He has withdrawn the sense of His presence in order for her to awaken and pursue Him. Even though there is a tangible residual anointing upon her heart and hand, we see her passion has cooled. She has become satisfied with the shadows and must once again be drawn away! Though traces of His presence can be sensed, the sad fact is in many places He is no longer desired even unwelcome. Jesus calls to this complacent, self-righteousness Bride with no desire or sense of need for His manifest presence, to open her heart and allow Him in once again. In need of a fresh filling of His Spirit, Jesus is speaking to a lukewarm Church, as He does in Revelation 3:20, "Behold, I stand at the door and knock..." To those who will allow, He will once again come in.

Out of the Shadows

Throughout Song of Solomon we see the true Bride is one whose desire is to be drawn out of the shadows, for the shadows to flee away and disappear. We like the Bride in Song of Solomon should have the desire to come out of the shadows. Shadows are the images, the types, symbols, signs, previews, but not the real thing *(Hebrews 8:1–5; 10:1)*. They are religious practices like those the Israelites were given that could only point to Christ and His redemptive work. We no longer need settle for mere shadows even though they may offer a sense of refreshment, security, holiness, or peace, for they are what they are, substitutes for the real, that which is without real substance as we read of in *Colossians 2:16–17*. They are mere images, representative figures, resemblances, often illusions, or even worse, idols.

The lesson from Song of Solomon is that there is more than the drawing to salvation, His drawing of the Bride is more than a one-time event, it is a continual leading along the path, a progression, and a journey of encounters between the Bride and Christ. In past Church history as today, we see people being drawn out; we see an awakening. We are witnessing today many reawakened and answering the call to come out of old and empty man-made ways and traditions back into intimate relationship with Jesus, back to a gospel lifestyle full of power and glory. One demonstrated in the lost, deceived, and hurting world.

This period of separation, or as we refer to it, *The Church Age*, I believe is alluded to further in *Song 6:1–2* through the question: *"Where has your beloved gone?"* He has departed to His Father's House to prepare a place for her. This, it appears, refers to that which Peter writes in *2 Peter 3*, where is the promise of His return? The answer lies in chapters 6–8 where we see He no longer calls her; He takes her, after which she accompanies Him in His return.

His Return to the Father

Chapter 3 begins with the idea of separation and ends with a reference to the day of betrothal. The middle section, while on the surface describes a wedding procession, in light of our discussion, it is a depiction of Bride's witness of the Bridegroom. An ongoing witness that began some 2000 years ago, one of the Bride's responsibilities as the Bridegroom is away preparing a home for the Bride.

> *John 14:1–4(KJV)*
> *Let not your heart be troubled: ye believe in God, believe also in me.*
> *2 In my Father's house are many mansions: if it were not so, I would have told you. I go to prepare a place for you.3 And if I go and prepare a place for*

*you, I will come again, and **receive** you unto myself;*
that where I am, there ye may be also. 4 And whither
I go ye know, and the way ye know.

The word "receive" is the transliterated Greek word *paralam-banó (par-al-am-ban'-o)* meaning to take or receive. It is a verb used for to take one's betrothed to his home.

As was said in the introduction in the Hebrew culture of Jesus day it was common after the betrothal ceremony for the Bridegroom to return to his father's house to prepare the home in which the couple would live. As he would leave the Bride, the Bridegroom would make a statement promising not only to build their future home but likewise proclaim the promise to come back and take her from her father's residence, and carry her away to their home and life together. Unknown to the bridegroom was when his father would give the permission for him to return for his bride. Only after the father was satisfied that all the necessary preparations had been completed would he say to his son something along the lines of: now, you may go take your bride and bring her home. Jesus of course refers to this when He states of His return that neither He nor the angles in heaven, likewise no man, knows when He will return, only the Father knows when He will release the Son to take His bride *(Matthew 2427–44: Mark 13:32; Luke 21:34–36).*

Psalm 45: The Wedding Psalm of the Sanctified

Verse 10 of *Psalm 45* speaks of those to be received; it is a portrait of Ruth who left her family, country, culture, people, and language. Like Ruth we must forget about our past, abandon ourselves in Him, we must abandon the familiar, even the traditions. We must cut off old loyalties, those things that compete with the relationship. We cannot allow ourselves to be held back by those who have no passion; by those who chose not to follow Him if we are to be the Bride described in *Psalm 45*, one who stands with her King, standing in and with Him in His glory, majesty, and eternal power. This Bride cannot compromise or remain neutral, she must choose a side, in fact, she will by default detach from one side or the other.

In *Psalm 45:10* the Bride is told, "Forget your Father's House" for us, this means following Jesus, cutting off our old nature in Adam becoming Kingdom cultured as opposed to worldly cultured. The Bride, who has accepted His invitation of sanctification and redemption, is now one of purity. As we see in *Song 4:7–8,* she is called out from the nations, and peoples who dwell not in covenant with Him. She has come down or separated herself from the influences of culture (Mountains). He has called her out from Lebanon. Lebanon, known for it beauty and pleasant fragrances *(Song 4:11),* represents worldly enticements and behaviors that promise to provide for fleshly, sensual, even intellectual pleasure. Remember we are separated from the life in which Adam subjected mankind. Adam chose the knowledge of good and evil, the power to choose for himself moral standards of right and wrong, thus to sit as God, as his own authority. This sin of rebellion severed the relationship with God, subjecting all mankind to death and curse. Since she has chosen another path, accepting His redemption, and now deemed sinless and blameless *(Song 4:7),* she must separate herself from the Leopards, that which is stained by sin, and from dens of the lions, dangerous beast of prey lying in wait to devour, hunting her life and soul, for we know bad company corrupts good character *(1 Corinthians 15:33).*

Come with Me, He says, for she cannot do so alone, she must choose His way, His influence, His authority, for as we know, it is not by power or might, it is not by sheer will power, it is only by the power of Holy Spirit that she, by grace, becomes transformed. A transformation, seen in *Song of Solomon 4,* that takes place as she answers His call to come to Him, turning her attention and affections toward Him. In chapter 1 she is dark, she has not kept her own vineyard, she has lived a life unworthy of the King, but oh what a change takes place, look at how the King sees her in *Song 4:9–11,* what a tremendous difference her choice to follow Him has made *(Song 4:12–15)!*

This is the path and pattern we all must choose if we are to accept His offer and price of Betrothal, if we are to follow Him by sanctifying our lives unto Him, and if we are to be joined to Him one day in that marriage. Truly following Jesus has been a challenge for the Church from the beginning. In many ways His Bride has failed to follow or to listen to Him. Jesus said My Sheep know My voice, but ask many who claim to be Christian and they will confess an inability to hear God, even to the point of saying those who claim to do so are insane. This leads me to believe that many so-called Christians are so in name only but lack actual relationship with Christ. Jesus died that we might have relationship, however as said, man has sought merely a religion, a religion of dogmas and ritualistic observances that make them feel holy, and that many have killed in order to protect. Sadly much of which are merely forms of Godliness, as Paul said, that deny or reject the true power of the Faith to which they claim to adhere. Christianity has become much like the description of Israel in the day of Moses seen in *Psalm 81*. Without relationship, without obedience, so too today we often play the "Grace Card" in order to justify living un-sanctified lives. Grace is a wonderful thing but what Grace is not is a license to determine for our self what is good and what is evil. We, like Adam and Eve, may attempt to do so but only God has that authority and we cannot assume that He has ordained our opinion as to what does or does not constitute sin. Too many so-called Christians today are like the 7 women in *Isaiah 4:1* who want Jesus in name only, desiring to receive the full benefit package of salvation without eating His food or wearing His clothes, in effect rejecting the terms of His sacrifice, not accepting His righteousness. Jesus made it dreadfully clear that this is unacceptable *(Matthew 7:22–23)*. To be the Bride, Jesus must know us and we must know Him, a term suggesting the intimate knowledge of a covenantal marital relationship.

What has happened in much of Christianity is the same as was with Adam and Eve; they lost their intimate personal relationship with God when the enemy planted seeds of doubt and unbelief in their thoughts. Saying in effect: God never said that, Jesus never said that, Jesus never addressed that issue in the New Testament. Yet we must remember Jesus is the Word of God; what is said in the Old Covenant is Jesus speaking. The fact that God deals with mankind differently in the dispensation of Grace does not mean that His opinion of sin or that which constitutes sin has changed for the Word says God does not change. God's character, nature, and opinion are the same today, yesterday, and forever *(Malachi 3:6; Hebrews 13:8).*

CHAPTER 4
Assuming The Nature of the King

Song of Solomon chapter 4 is a continuation of the Sanctification period and description of the sanctified Bride. The indication being this period is one of length. Here we see the Bride's defining moment, her becoming who she is in Him, becoming the image and reflection of the Bridegroom *(Ephesians 5:27)*. It is His word(s) spoken to her that bless and define her. It is who she is in His eyes, in His judgment.

Defining the line between sanctimonious religion and true relationship, the true Bride is wholly devoted to Christ. She is nothing like those who by word, but not in heart, proclaim to be called by His name, including those who Jesus said will say to Him: We have healed, cast out demons, and prophesied in Your name, those to whom He will say: depart from Me for I never knew you.

Mt. Hermon

Song of Solomon 4:8 (KJV)
8 Come with me from Lebanon, my spouse,...
look from the top of Amana, from the top of Shenir
and Hermon,

In addition to that which was previously stated concerning Mt. Hermon are a few more considerations of particular interest to point out. First Mt. Hermon is the highest point in Israel; second it is where the Jordan River is said to begin. The Bridegroom says: come from the summit, from the top of Mt. Hermon. Summit here is the Hebrew *rosh (roshe)* meaning the top, the head, master, ruler, place, rank, position in society, etc. As said it is the starting place of the Jordan River. The Jordan "Yarden" in Hebrew means descend or to descend, it is the lowest river in elevation of the world. This river makes what would be a dry desert valley, fruitful. It terminates in the Dead Sea, the lowest point on Earth, a place where nothing lives and nothing escapes. Having no outlet it represents death, the grave. As we know the last enemy to be defeated or put under Jesus's feet will be death. As prophesied in *Ezekiel 47*, when The Messiah reigns the Dead Sea will be restored to life, and be full of life.

> *Joshua 1:11*
> *Pass through the host, and command the people, saying, Prepare you victuals; for within three days ye shall pass over this Jordan, to go in to possess the land, which the Lord your God giveth you to possess it.*

To be restored to life, to inherit eternal life we must likewise pass or cross over, or according to the definition of the Hebrew word used, *abar (aw-bar')*, meaning to alienate, alter, or overcome. As we saw concerning the Mikvah the betrothed Bride must become alienated, or by definition she must transfer ownership or legal rights from one person to another. She must alter her life, overcome certain things, she must descend by transferring her rights and affections from one to another.

Clearly the Jordan represents humbling. It is Jesus who humbled Himself coming down from heaven to become a man. In the same manner, it is we who must humble ourselves, we must cross over, we must go through Him, through a conversion, if we are to conquer death, and enter into the promise of God.

In chapter 4 we see the result of conversion. As we read over and over again in the Song, once a person has accepted Christ's purchase price, that person is clean, pure, and able to be baptized and filled with the Holy Spirit. Now fruitful, this crowned Bride is an equipped army, sanctified and called to live continually so in the time of separation.

The words the Bridegroom uses to speak of His Bride point to this idea of conversion and sanctification. As said, she possesses Dove's eyes, which again refers to the Holy Spirit within her. In speaking of her hair, the implication is she, to her glory, is covered by and submitted to His authority (*see 1 Corinthians 11:1–15*). This idea of hair relating to sanctification is also seen in the vow of the Nazirite, one whose uncut hair symbolized his separation and dedication to God *(Judges 16:17)*. Her hair is like a flock of goats. Goat hair was one of the fabrics used for the covering of the tabernacle *(Exodus 26:7–8)*. The Tabernacle itself covered by fire and cloud was not only the dwelling place of God among the Israelites; it symbolized the Messiah. His Bride, the Church, currently His temple, is the dwelling place of the Lord, She is under His authority, and is the possession of Christ by virtue of having brought herself under His covering.

> *Song of Solomon 7:5 (KJV)*
> *5 Thine head upon thee is like Carmel, and the hair of thine head like purple; the king is held in the galleries.*

Even more emblematic is His statement, "your hair is like purple" or better understood from the Hebrew word *"argaman,"* red-purple. Purple, as we will discuss further with the sapphire, refers to a King, and red or crimson of course, blood. We see then she is covered by kingly blood. As *Revelation 1:5* says the blood of Jesus has washed us from sin.

He then describes her teeth as like sheep coming up from the washing to indicate her baptism, her Mikvah. We can better understand this by examining washing. Washing is the Hebrew noun *hārahṣāh or rachtsah (rakh-tsaw')* meaning simply, washing. It is the feminine of Hebrew noun *rachats (rakh'-ats)* meaning a washbowl, a bathing place, and is derived from the verb *rachats (raw-khats')* meaning to bathe. This word is used in *Psalm 26* by David to describe innocence, David washing his hands making him innocent and in *Isaiah 4:4* to speak of cleansing from filthiness, Zechariah also uses a related word to describe filthy garments and iniquity exchanged for righteousness. *Ezekiel 16* is another example where God washed the Israelites in the Red Sea as they were born as a nation, their birth.

What we see here is, as a part of her re-birth the Bride is washed, made innocent, cleansed of all unrighteousness, just as we see of the Church in *Acts 22:16; Hebrews 10:22; Revelation 1:5,* and especially *Ephesians 5:26.*

> *Ephesians 5:26–27 (KJV)*
> *26 That he might sanctify and cleanse it with the washing of water by the word, 27 That he might present it to himself a glorious church, not having spot, or wrinkle, or any such thing; but that it should be holy and without blemish.*

Washed by His blood and His word, having partaken of and eaten of Him in Song 2:3, her heart has been made pure, and from the abundance of the purity of her heart come her pure and unde-filed, clean words. She has become fruitful and blessed.

That she is fruitful is seen in Solomon's use of the word Pomegranate. Pomegranates are rife with metaphor, first is that they possess a crown. Pomegranates represent fruitfulness and are part of the fall fruit harvest, the Feast of Tabernacles. They were used as a wine and as a medicine. Their crimson color suggests a blushing Bride, and their "bleeding" juice speaks again of blood. And quite interestingly, their representation was sown into the hem of the Priestly garments.

Since withering pomegranates indicated God's judgment and a lack of joy and rejoicing in *Joel 1:12,* conversely flourishing pome-granates then symbolize joy, rejoicing, and the absence of God's judg-ment. In other words she can rejoice in that she has been reconciled to God in her Bridegroom, Jesus, and will not be found subject to

God's wrath but rather in that day, a participant in the marriage supper of the Lamb!

The Bridal Army

She is not merely blessed; she is a prosperous and equipped army. Her neck like the Tower of David, David meaning loved, and tower, *migdal or migdalah*, from *gadal* meaning to become great, to make large (in various senses, as in body, mind, estate or honor), to advance, exceed, to become excellent. Again this points to her change of status from a slave in bondage to a position of authority through His name.

This tower, presumed not to be the one you see in Jerusalem, nevertheless, was an armory built by David as a weapons cache. Being the place his great warriors stored their armor, perhaps trophies of battle, it signified both warriors and their honor. We see then the Bride is not merely majestic, but a victorious warrior! David was a man of war, his son Solomon a man of peace. One day this Bride of Jesus, the Prince of Peace and King of Kings, victorious over the enemy, her warfare being complete will lay down her weapons. And not to be forgotten, as *Proverbs 18:10* says, the name of the Lord is a Strong Tower where the righteous run to and are safe. And if her neck is a strong tower, it has then lifted her head and eyes focusing them upon Him!

To reiterate, described in verses 6–8 is sanctification, or her period of separation. In verse 11 Her purity and righteousness. In verses 12–15 Solomon will describe her fragrance, which we will address in detail, a fragrance illustrating her status in the time of betrothal, and her reflection and representation of Him as she radiates His character and nature. All of which we read in verse 16 are dependent upon the Holy Spirit, the life giving breath of the God we need in order to be filled with, and release His anointing *(see John 20:22).*

A Ravished Heart, Prayer and Worship

Song of Solomon 4:7, 9 (KJV)
*   7 Thou art all fair, my love; there is no spot*
in thee.
*   9 Thou hast ravished my heart, my sister, my*
spouse; thou hast ravished my heart with one of
thine eyes, with one chain of thy neck.

Do you see how the Lord sees you as His Bride? He sees you as pure, undefiled, and without sin. Does this grace, as it is known in the New Covenant, make it ok to sin or disobey God's rules, to live by our own desires? NO. Because such a great love has been given freely to us we should have a strong desire to love Him in return. We know to love Him is to obey Him, as stated in the discussion of Agápē. Love in the Hebrew cultural sense refers to how one treats and protects a privileged gift, therefore we should have no desire to do anything that would hurt or destroy that love relationship.

What about this word ravished? Ravish is to overwhelm with emotions, to enrapture, to delight beyond measure, to take away ones heart such as a woman when she captivates or opens the deep recesses of a man's heart so that he desires a pure intimacy with her. He desires to give to her, to cover and protect her, to give himself to her and only her. It is covenant.

We have ravished His heart. As men and women we want the one we love and desire to respond to our love and desire. We want to hear them say our name. We want to hear them say our name. We want their desire to be for us. We want to take them in our arms. We want them to run to us. We want them to run into our arms. We want to be with the one we love; we want to spend time with them. We want to share our deepest desires and our deepest emotions. We desire to share the depths of our heart and soul with each other. Husbands it would be good for you to remember the earliest days of your relationship with your wife. The days your love first began to develop. Remember how being apart made you cry out in your soul longing for her. Longing to be with her. Remember how separation left a void in your heart one more than you thought you could bear. This is Jesus's heart and desire for His bride. We have ravished His heart; we consume His thoughts. His passion and desire for us to be in His presence was so strong He left heaven and His glory to come and find us.

He was willing to suffer rejection, pain, humiliation, and die for that relationship just so we can experience His touch not only daily, but also for eternity. What a powerful demonstration of Love. He sought us and now we must seek Him and respond to His love. If we will come or draw close to God He will come close to us. He made the first move by sending His son in love to open the door. The curtain or veil separating man from God has been torn through Jesus crucifixion *Hebrews 10:19–21*. Now we must in turn open the door of our heart to Him. He is jealous for us. Are we giving and surrendering ourselves to Him? Do we hunger and thirst for Him? Those who hunger and thirst will be filled to satisfaction.

The Lord is ready to touch, heal, and fill our soul. He is here to heal and comfort our pain, sorrow, and infirmities. He has done everything He can do now we must respond to Him. He longs to fill us with His presence. What would you not do to comfort and strengthen the one you love, what would you not do to see them joyful and happy. The Lord likewise wants to touch our soul, our wounds, our pains, and our infirmities. He has done everything He can do; now we must respond. Now we must receive.

The Lord desires to take you into his Most Holy Place, to take you deeper, beyond just a superficial or surface level relationship. He desires to give you and encounter and experience with Him. His desire for you is far greater than you can understand. He is ready to reveal Himself to you and to reveal His power, glory, His secret counsel, and the depths of knowledge of His Word. He wants to reveal the Power of his Word and to give you a revelation of His Name, the very name, which you are called!

Her Fragrance

In Song of Solomon chapter 4 we see the declaration of the Bridegroom, Jesus's desire and longing for communion with His Church. The Bride alluded to in verse 12 is as a garden enclosed, her soul and spirit housed in this mortal corruptible body of flesh has yet to be clothed in incorruption and immorality *(1 Corinthians 15:35–54; 2 Corinthians 5:1–8)*. Also indicating there has, as of yet, been no consummation of the marriage, signifying they are still in the period of betrothal, the time He is absent "preparing a place for her." What we also notice is that as His Church looks to Him, as she worships, His heart is captivated or taken, in other words she receives His heart. Though the two are physical separated, chapter 4, as does *Psalm 2, 2* describes the Lord enthroned or inhabiting her praise. His presence is within and fills her heart each time she turns her focus and attention upon Him. Through worship, the Church is able to radiate outwardly all that He is and has made her to be.

Let us consider her fragrance in *Song of Solomon Song of Solomon 4:10–16* noticing the similarities to that of His as described in chapter 3 verse 6. The fragrances emitting from the Bride are deep in meaning and significance. These fragrances, along with the plants and manner in which the scents are extracted; represent the work and sacrifice of Jesus on the Cross. The scents or aromas carried by the Bride are the product or results of His sacrifice.

As we examine these fragrances we will explore the individual symbolic meaning behind them. First and foremost when considering the fragrances, the plants, their manner of extraction or production, and the release of such fragrances, we must do so from the viewpoint of love. It was Christ love for mankind that He allowed Himself to be made a sacrifice and it is from love that the Bride allows herself to release these fragrances in and unto those in the world.

It is important to note that listed here are nine fragrances of the Bride, fragrances only made possible in and through Jesus. Nine symbolically suggest the Holy Spirit, the nine gifts of the Spirit, and the nine fruits of the Spirit. Spiritual fruit is the evidence of spiritual growth and maturity. Mature fruit speaks of that which is ready to be harvested, partaken of, and that which will bless, satisfy, nourish, and bring life and health.

Also of note is in verse 13 of chapter 4 He speaks of the fragrances of her plants as opposed to those of her garments in verse 11. The word plant now becomes important to our understanding. Plant, Hebrew *shelach,* can be defined as missile (of attack), weapon, defense, or sprout. Sprout being an outgrowth or Branch, I capitalize branch here for the obvious connotation of Jesus. In addition, *shelach* comes from the Hebrew word *shalach* meaning to send. Prophetically, these plants are on one level symbolic of the physical body of Jesus, and on another of His Bride, the Church, which as we know is His body.

Let us now consider the various plants, the substances they produce, and the violent manner by which the substance and fragrances are obtained. Jesus experienced violence against both His body and soul and likewise have many who are of His body. As we know the violence Jesus suffered was actually a weapon that defeated death, hell, the grave, Satan, and all the powers of darkness. So too can the acts of physical and emotional violence against those who are or become "His Body", those things the enemy intended to kill, steal, and destroy them through, become weapons against evil. Becoming the substance of healing, pleasantness and restoration as they are sent to others in suffering.

Lebanon, in verse 11 of chapter 4 her garments emit the scent of Lebanon. Lebanon, used here in a positive sense, leads us back to the detailed discussion of the palanquin. The implication being, emanating from the Bride is the fragrance of Jesus crucifixion, which of course from her position is the fragrance of life. Lebanon is known in scripture for its trees in particular the Cedar. We see then the scent released from her garments is exuding the odor of cedar. Solomon used the cedars of Lebanon in the construction of the Temple; the obvious connection here is to the Church being the Temple of the Holy Spirit *(1 Corinthians 6:19)*. The implication being the Bride is one who will inherit incorruption. Furthermore, Lebanon from its snow-covered mountains has come to imply white or whiteness.

And, considering the root words from which Lebanon is derived, we have a veiled description of the Bride's heart, mind, inner being, and will, in other words her soul having been cleansed and purified; He, Jesus our High Priest, has pronounced His Bride clean. *See Isaiah 61:10; Zechariah 3:3—5; 1 Corinthians 15:42; Revelation 3:5, 18; 19:7—8.*

Henna is symbolic of the ransom, redemption, and propitiation of the Bride. Henna, *or* camphire is the Hebrew *kopher,* figuratively meaning ransom or redemption price, the price of life. *NAS Exhaustive Concordance* says *kopher* is from the same word origin as *Kephir*, a lion and *Kephir* is from *kaphar* meaning to appease. *Strong's Exhaustive Concordance* defines *kaphar* as to make an atonement, to expiate, cancel, forgive, be merciful, pardon, purge (away), to reconcile or make reconciliation, propitiate, and to cover. According to *Fausset's Bible Dictionary* its dry leaves yield red oil that was and is still used for staining women's nails[1]. When we read *Song of Solomon 1:14* this idea of propitiation becomes most interesting. Here the Bride declares Him to be to her a cluster of Henna blooms, a royal king who is her propitiation, as we know Jesus, the lion of the tribe of Judah, was made by the Father, our propitiation *(Romans 3:25; 1 John 2:2; 4:10).*

Jesus sent by the Father to satisfy the offense between Man and God, appeased the wrath of God for any who accept Him as their redeemer, as the one who paid the ransom price to become their propitiation, making them by His blood, the ransomed, redeemed, and reconciled unto God.

Spikenard or Nard produced from the *Nard* plant consist many spikes springing from one root. Two ways we can view the spikes of this plant. One, the nails that pierced the hands and feet of Jesus and two, Jesus the root Branch, and His precious Bride-Church the many spikes for which He paid the most costly price.

In Hebrew Spikenard represents the precious, the costly, anointing, and worship. Spikenard oil, as we know, was used by Mary to anoint Jesus for burial in *John 12:3–8*, thus suggesting, anointing, death and burial. In regard to worship, Spikenard oil was kept sealed in an alabaster box that had to be broken in order to access the substance and release the fragrance. Precious and very costly its oil diffuses a strong perfume, one which filled the house as Mary, in an act of worship, used it to anoint Jesus for His crucifixion *(John 12:3–7)*.

As we know some of our most precious worship comes in times of brokenness, in times it cost us the most to do so. As we, the Bride, open our hearts in surrender, releasing our lives to and for Him, through our spirit and truth worship, we allow the precious fragrance of Christ to be released in and through us. And as when Mary anointed Christ, the very fragrance of this act of worship penetrated the very atmosphere and garments of those in the room, so too will and costly worship impact the atmosphere into which it is released. Praise is also our gift back to Him, our gift of bringing glory to His name. The praises, the worship of His Bride will release the fragrance of His glory capable of saturating any who are nearby.

I read somewhere that the root Hebrew word for Nard is light. Not finding this in my usual sources of reference, I plugged this word into the Hebrew to English dictionary site *Morfix*. What I found, though perhaps not hermeneutically applicable, was interesting.

> Nard: נֵרְדְ
> נ nun
> ר resh: law defendant
> דְ Dalet: in ancient pictographs represents a door
> נֵרְדְ nard, spikenard: to descend, to go down ; to decrease ; to lessen, to diminish
> רְדְ said of night or darkness: to fall
> נֵר Candle-Oil Lamp: light

As I viewed the individual letters the "Dalet" and "Resh" in particular stood out. Dalet the door represents both Jesus the door and the door of our heart that we must open to receive Christ, again an act of worship, and Resh, we who are a defendant, an offender in need of an advocate. By removing either the first or last letter to see what might be conveyed by the potential root words in nard, I came up with a something I would like to suggest from this word. We are a defendant accused by the Law, one we know is guilty, a person in darkness in need of light who must humble themselves and accept the "Light" and must walk in the light as He is and is in the Light *(John 1:1–14; 3:19; 8:12 1 John 1:7)*. And then, as we will see in chapter 5 it is the Bride on trial by a world walking in darkness in need of an advocate, helper, and comforter, the Paraclete!

Saffron, which produces a deep yellow powder, indicates Jesus's Church becoming a Reflection of His glory. Saffron is said to be the Crocus sativusis, a purple flowering plant bearing up to four flowers, each with three vivid crimson stigmas. Saffron produces a spice, which has long been among the world's most costly by weight. It contains a carotenoid pigment, which imparts a rich golden-yellow hue to dishes and textiles. One thing I found in researching saffron was a report stating multiple scientific studies concluded that saffron supplementation improved symptoms in patients with mild to moderate depression *[52]* as well as major depressive disorders *[51]²*.

Look for a moment at the golden-yellow hue, the shimmering-gold if you will.

> *Psalm 68:13 (NKJV)*
> *13 Though (When) you lie down among the sheepfolds,*
> *You will be like the wings of a dove covered with silver,*
> *And her feathers with yellow gold*

In chapter 1 we saw the fatherless Bride join herself to His Flock or Sheepfold. The dove, as stated, describes those belonging to The Lord, and silver points to the redeemed. David, in *Psalm 68,* in his praise to God the Father to the fatherless, describes the redeemed as wings of the dove with yellow, or in its Hebrew context *shimmering gold* feathers. As *Psalm 45:9* indicates, as we His Bride stand in the presence of The King of glory we are covered in gold.

Of particular interest are the crimson stigmas or *pistils* of this plant, which produce the flowers from which its fragrance is extracted. Stigma or stigmata, as we know, refer to the wounds of Christ. Stigma, defined as a mark of disgrace, a point on the skin that bleeds when one is under great emotional distress, or the labeling of one as a criminal, all of which we read in the Gospels, describe Christ as He endured judgment and crucifixion. Purchased with Jesus's blood, a most costly price for a most valuable Bride, she is healed and made whole not only physically but likewise in the mind and soul, for He has given His beloved the covering garment of praise to defeat the spirit of heaviness *(Isaiah 61:3)*. The Lord indicating to His Church you are set free from sorrow and depression. You have been redeemed, purchased by His power and glory. When you praise, when you declare his word and His greatness, heaviness no longer has dominion and control over your life. He has paid the price, He is your garment of praise; He is your deliverer. He has surrounded His Bride with the song of deliverance, the power of Praise.

Psalm 32:7
 7 Thou art my hiding place (covering, pro-
tection); thou shalt preserve me from trouble; thou
shalt compass me about with songs of deliverance.
Selah.

Calamus, *qaneh* branches, or Sweet Cane, is a reedlike plant much jointed and very fragrant when bruised[3]. *Qaneh* is from the Hebrew *qanah*, meaning to buy or acquire, and expresses symbolic meanings such as owner, possession, sold, purchased, or redeemed. Jesus is the vine we are His branches. This reed or rod thus expresses redemption, the redeemed, and bruising. I also suggest, as we will see, it represents humility.

Focusing on reed(s) we should first think of Moses, saved from death by being placed in a bulrush "reed" ark, his mother laying the basket with baby in the reeds of the river, a child rescued that would later, as a type of Christ, lead the Israelites out of bondage. Jesus, who was sold for thirty pieces of silver, laid down His life to redeem

His Bride, His purchased possession from every nation, tribe, and tongue.

Reeds resemble a rod and portray various symbolic meanings. The Calamus, somewhat of a weak plant, bends or lays flat under gust of wind yet is able bounce back to an upright position. Need I remind us of the Holy Spirit coming as a rushing mighty wind? Are we one who will bow in deference or surrender to His will and presence? As *James 4:10* states, when we humble ourselves in the sight of the Lord He will lift us up.

Yielding and submissive Calamus is a picture of humility *(see also Isaiah 58:5)*. Jesus will not crush those who humble themselves in surrender to Him as He said in *Matthew 12:20* a bruised reed I will not break. The Calamus also represents our weakness as well as Jesus being made weak as it were by becoming flesh. Bending and weak from the weight of sin, we were once crushed under its burden, guilt, and shame, however Jesus by His grace has strengthened us making us once again upright before God.

We, like the reed, are fragile, weak, easily swayed by the winds, easily broken down. Bruised, without strength, wounded, rejected, perhaps having suffered injury, misuse, or abuse, none of which with Jesus however are permanent or irreparable. Jesus was rejected and bruised, on our behalf. He knows our pain, our sorrow, and broken heart. He came so that He might repair and heal the broken hearted *(Isaiah 61:1; Luke 4:18)*.

This reed, which must be beaten, bruised, and crushed to powder in order to release its fragrance, then represents Jesus; bruised for our iniquities having made His Church a pleasant fragrance to the Father. There is no longer any guilt, condemnation, or fault to be found in those who submit to His authority, His true Church-Bride *(Song. 4:7; Jude 1:24)*.

In the humility of Jesus, the bruised Branch, we discover another symbolic meaning in the reed as it represents a staff, or scepter, the rod of authority. As the soldiers mocked Jesus as a king a reed was placed in His hand as a derogatory gesture of His weak kingdom and authority. Then, placing a crown of thorns on His head, they took back the reed beating Him with it on the head *(Matthew 27:29–30)*.

This we have addressed in the discussion of *Solomon in Song 3:11* speaking of Christ crowned on the day of his betrothal.

Cinnamon, a spice used in the anointing oil, is a symbol of holiness and righteousness. Cinnamon or *qinnamon,* consist of profuse white blossoms with bark in upright rolls expresses the idea of uprightness. One of the most absolutely intriguing aspects of the cinnamon plant is how it is grown and harvested. A few short years after planted it will be cut off at ground level. From one branch and one root it will produce twelve shoots. Does this at all sound familiar? Jesus, as Daniel was told, would be cut off but not for Himself. And as we know, found His Church through twelve Apostles. And yet there is more. When harvested the outer bark of the plant is scraped away, the outer covering is then hammered (beaten) and broken apart revealing the inner cane. We have already discussed Jesus being beaten but what about the Church? Jesus said He is the Rock, the chief cornerstone, upon which any who fall would be broken *(Matthew 21:42–44).*

Cinnamon then is a portrait of the flesh and the spirit, the outer man and inner man, of putting off the old and putting on the new man, of the old fleshly minded outer man crucified with Christ in order that the new man, made alive, might be released and strengthened through the Holy Spirit *(Romans 6:6; 2 Corinthians 4:16–18; Ephesians 3:16–17, 4:22).*

Frankincense called pure incense; represents purity. Frankincense is from a root word meaning whiteness and when burned produces a white smoke. Frankincense, bitter and glittering, is extracted by making cuts in the plant's bark wherefrom, dripping out as tears, pours a substance bitter to the taste yet sweet to the smell. Symbolizing the bitterness of the Cross, making His Church, as is He, a sweet smelling aroma to God *(Ephesians 5:2; 2 Corinthians 2:14–15). Easton's Bible Dictionary* states that when burnt it emits a fragrant odor…the incense became a symbol of the Divine name *(Malachi 1:11; Song. 1:3),* an emblem of prayer *(Psalm 141:2; Luke 1:10; Revelation 5:8; 8:3),* and worship[4]; thus it represents that which is accepted by God. It was part of the incense placed before the Ark of the Covenant in the Holy of Holies, the place of God's presence. It was part of the gifts given to Jesus at His birth.

Myrrh is symbolic of suffering love, passion, awakening, healing, self-sacrifice, self-denial, and the bitterness of death to self and one's own will, plan, purpose. Myrrh we will look at in detail as we discuss His awakening of the sleeping Bride.

Aloes refer to death, to Christ crucifixion and the Bride being crucified with Christ. In *John 19:39* Nicodemus brought aloe (pounded aloe-wood) to embalm the body of Christ.

Fausset's Bible Dictionary says aloes are an image for all that is lovely, fragrant, flourishing, and incorruptible *(Numbers 24:6; Song of Song of Solomon 4:14)*. In *Romans chapter 6, and chapters 7:4; and 8:10–11;* then again in *1 Corinthians 15:22* and *Galatians 2:20* Paul speaks of our crucifixion with Christ, our death to sin and its power and influence over us, of our betrothal to Jesus by such death, and of our resurrection and life. Peter likewise, in *1 Peter 1:4, 23,* speaks of our inheriting incorruption.

Chief spices refer to a_Bride prepared, to death, burial, and resurrection, and to be alive in Christ. *International Standard Bible Encyclopedia* renders this to be balsam or bosem (beh'-sem). Bosem comes from a root meaning to attract by desire, especially smell. It is mentioned as one of the ingredients appointed for the anointing oil. It is rendered as sweet spices in *Song 4:12*; and is the perfumes mentioned in *Esther 2:12*; This product from the balsam plant was used for preparing women for marriage in particular purifying the women who were to be presented to the King. It is also a spice also burnt at burial *(2 Chronicles 16:14)*.

> *John 19:40 (KJV)*
> *40 Then took they the body of Jesus, and wound it in linen clothes with the spices, as the manner of the Jews is to bury.*

I want to look at something in *Isaiah 11:3*.

> *Isaiah 11:3 (KJV)*
> *3 And shall make him of quick understanding*
> *in the fear of the Lord...*

Some translations render it "he will delight in," "his delight is in" or "his delight shall be in" the fear of the Lord. The word delight or quick understanding, transliterated from the Hebrew, is rendered, "and shall make him of living understanding in the fear of the Lord." The actual word וַהֲרִיחוֹ (wa·hă·rî·ḥōw) is the verb ruach, from which the noun Ruach, or Spirit, as in the Spirit of the Lord, is derived. This verb means to smell, it can also mean to perceive or touch. So one might suggest it is one of the five senses. Smell and perceive suggest a scent. Knowing, as we should, that the fear of the Lord is worship, which is submission, obedience, respect and honor of the Lord, is it possible, at least in principle, to suggest His fragrance and His Spirit reside in and upon those that worship Him? Likewise does a worshipping Bride receive His wisdom, knowledge, understanding, *perception, discernment*, might, and counsel? I am of the opinion that it is a distinct possibility, for as we know she is a Bride becoming as He is.

The Jacob Code

Jacob, Isaac's son, was recognized, or in this case judged the one to receive the blessing and inheritance of the firstborn by the feel and smell of the firstborn. Jacob smelled like, and had the touch of the firstborn. When we get beyond the obvious deception and integrity issue there is a principle behind this account, first we must realize when one is "in Christ" and Jesus is in fact their Lord, God, the Father, no longer sees their sin, He sees His Son, He sees them through the blood of Jesus. The Bride will smell like the first born, Jesus. She will not carry or emit the stench of death, Satan, or the world because she is and has sanctified herself, no longer wallowing in the pigsty of its views, opinions, and behaviors. No, she will be distinguished because she smells of Him. Intimacy with Him, His touch upon her, has caused her to look, smell, think, and act differently from the world.

The fragrance one emits will either reflect Jesus or Satan who is the fragrance of the world. Her lips and her words likewise will reflect Him not the other. Recognize the fragrance and lips of the enemy for they are: pride, arrogance, self-promoting, worldly ambition, bitter, hate, accusing, judgment and condemnation, fear, doubt and unbelief, questions, testing and accusing God or man. Therefore in chapters 4 and 7, He can say of her lips and mouth, they are scarlet, lovely, honey, milk, and wine.

Awake, O North Wind, An Outpouring of the Holy Spirit

North scripturally refers to the throne of heaven (*Job 37:22; Isaiah 14:13*), and wind, as we know, to the Holy Spirit. In chapter 4 verses 15 and 16 I believe we see a Bride calling out to heaven for an outpouring of the Holy Spirit that will awaken the sleeping Church renewing and reviving their relationship through the Spirit of God, the river of living water. It is the wind of Holy Spirit that releases her fragrance and only through the power of Holy Spirit can the Bride release His. As we read in *2 Corinthians 2:14* through the Bride's personal relationship and experience with Christ is diffused the fragrance of the knowledge "doctrine and wisdom" of Christ be it the aroma of death or life as she emits the character and nature of Christ.

Jesus promoted the Father, not Himself. The Holy Spirit promotes Jesus. He reflects, emits, represents, and takes that which belongs to Christ and declares it to the Church. The Church in turn can, should, and will do likewise through the power of Holy Spirit.

The question we must ask ourselves is: how many fragrances do I emit? The Bride, as she receives and worships Him *(Song of Solomon 1:12–13; Psalm 45:11–12)*, becomes the fragrance of Christ, who we see is perfumed with myrrh, frankincense, aloes, and cassia as noted in *Song of Solomon 3:6;* and *Psalm 45:8.* The Bride becomes the fragrance of life and of death as Paul makes known in *2 Corinthians 2:15–16.* However, this fragrance of Christ diffused from our life will be perceived differently from one individual to another. Some will receive it, by others it will be refused. To those who despise and reject Jesus we are an offense, a repugnant odor that must be eliminated. To those whose hearts are open ready and willing to accept Christ, we, if we are willing, are an instrument of the Holy Spirit from whom springs a fountain of living water, a fragrance that brings life.

CHAPTER 5
The Bride Awakened

Chapter 5 of Song of Solomon is a prophetic look into the Church Age, in particular the laborers and harvest of the Last Days. A harvest that begins with Christ awakening and healing the Bride resulting in her subsequent witness of Him by answering the world's question of who is He.

In verse 1 we read, He comes into His garden, that is her heart. He has eaten and drunk of that which the Father ordained, that to which He agreed from before the foundation of the world, which is His suffering love, the price He paid for His Bride, "The Church." An offer made available to any who will accept it, an offer to exchange one's sin for His righteousness. An offer and possibility to exchange one's suffering for His healing and peace; to obtained life from His death and resurrection. This recurring message throughout the Song is one that must be repeated over and over again until it has been spoken to all the nations of the world.

In verse 2–3, we see Jesus reaching out to His Church, knocking at the door of her heart, however, many like the Bride we see here, perhaps even a bit self-righteous, say "I am clean"; I am good to go, my eternity is secure. A Church, as we have seen over the centuries, full of those who have lost their first love an their passion for Jesus, many of who have become unresponsive, dispassionate, disinterested, and unenthusiastic toward Him.

Described in verses 4–8 is an awakening, a restoration of the Bride's passion and fire, a renewed first love if you will, a renewed desire for His presence. Illustrated within these lines is a healing; an outpouring of the Holy Spirit leading to an outpouring of her worship, one that many, especially those with a religious spirit, will despise and persecute. Yet no persecution will stop or quench this revival fire. The Bride's praise and worship will not be silenced.

Depicted in verse 9 is the day in which we live, the day of awakening and revival. The world questions the Church, "Why is your god different than all others"? They say: "He is the same as all the rest, He is just one of many, He is just a man, why should we seek Him, why should we believe in Him, why should we follow or obey Him"?

As we enquire into into verses 10–16, we see not only the Bride's praise and worship; we see described a prophetic evangelism in the last days. An outpouring occurring as the "Church," both men and women, young and old alike begin to release the awakening and healing. *"Anointed"* with myrrh on their hands, they carry His authority and anointing demonstrating the Kingdom of God in the world around them.

The Sleeping Bride

He clothed Himself in humanity that we might be clothed in Him. In Song 5:3 we see the Bride has exchanged her garments for His. Exchanged her self-righteousness "Filthy Rags" for His holiness and righteousness. In *Zechariah 3:3–4* filthy garments speak of iniquity; yet in *Isaiah 61:10* we see one rejoicing as a Bride adorned, clothed by the Lord, in salvation and righteousness. The Bride whose garments now emit the fragrance of Lebanon, she no longer carries the semblance of sweat, sin, and the curse, but the aroma of purity. Once again made pleasing and acceptable to God. Yet over time, day by day the concerns of life began to consume her time and attention, weary she became a sleeping Bride. Saying in effect; now isn't that enough? I don't want or need to go further, it is too extreme to show passion. Such an attitude has led her into indifference and complacency.

Complacent, she seems annoyed as He knocks on the door of her heart desiring intimacy. Proclaiming "I have" and indirectly "I am," I am good to go I am clean, I don't need you right now, I am clean and righteous. Solomon not only describes for us what we read over and over in the Old Testament of Israel in its relationship to God, he outlines so clearly how the Church in the dispensation of grace will and has grown cold toward Jesus, being as it were righteous, pure, and clean in its own eyes, by its own religious actions. Many having no desire for His presence, just as the Israelites of old, have become satisfied with the ceremonial while shunning the relational.

Clearly in chapter 5 of Song of Solomon, through the symbolism of her sleeping and the cold indifference that has gripped her soul, He, the King, has been away for some time. Making this, I believe, a prophetic dream of the "Church Age" for a long period of time appears to have passed. Today, can and will the Church awaken to His presence?

In one sense the condition of the sleeping Bride is described in the Church of Laodicea, the last mentioned, a foreshadow of the final, end of days Church, one who is lukewarm, self-righteous, and feels secure in her eternity, yet is deceived. Compromised in some way with the culture and environment surrounding them, they have even fallen prey to false teaching. It is in this day and this condition we see Jesus tenderly speaking to individual hearts, calling out to awaken His Bride to repentance, longing that they would once again allow His word and truth to govern their lives. His reproof reveals His love and desperation for His Bride. As it was in the early days of the Church, worldly outside influences such as Gnosticism, intellectualism, rationalism, philosophy, legalism, false mysticism, and immorality, etc. have infiltrated the Church. As Paul reveals in *Colossians 2:8–23* the Church has been defrauded and deceived by philosophy, the traditions of man, worldly principles, pride, false humility, an intellectualized gospel, and legalistic rules and regulations.

Having become intellectually enlightened, lukewarm, proud, self-sufficient, stale, and stagnant this form of Church became fluctuating, unstable, and inconsistent.

Always changing their opinions and standards (beliefs) to keep current with societal mores they are the Apostate "Zeitgeist" Church prophesied by Paul to come in the end *(2 Thessalonians 2:3)*. Full of religious pretense and appearance yet without substance, empty, and deceived, thinking they have or know it all, they worship with their mouth but in truth their heart is far from the Lord. In their false security, they imagine they are ok, good to go with God but they are not! Doing the minimum required, just enough of what they suppose pleases God by means of their liturgies and sacraments, in reality they misunderstand God completely, not recognizing the Lord actually desires not religion but relationship. And as with the wretched, poor, blind, and naked Church of Laodicea who received no commendation or praise from Christ; the admonition is the same, repent. Jesus, nevertheless, has not given up on them totally; the invitation remains available for them to return to Him. Even though they have shut Jesus out of their lives, He continues to seek them out to bring them back in. Jesus saying today the same as then: "As many as I love, I rebuke and chasten." His correction is proof He still loves them.

Like a broken-hearted husband, one ready to forgive her unfaithfulness, Jesus stands at the door of an unfaithful and departing Church. Knocking individually on the door of her heart, He sends out a plea to accept His terms of return just as they accepted and received His gift of Salvation.

Have you fallen asleep; are you one whose passion has cooled? When we experience times of cooling passion and we no longer feel eager for His presence we must endeavor to rekindle the fire knowing He seeks to awaken our passion.

What Happened while the Bride Slept?

In *Matthew 13:24–30, 36–43* Jesus tell us specifically what took place as the Bride slept; the enemy came in sowing tares within the Church. Tares are intentional, by design, and purposely sown by the enemy. Tares look like and pretend to be wheat but they are of another seed, a poison seed. Jesus, as He said in *John 12:24*, is the seed of the wheat, and Satan is the seed of the fatal and deceptive tares.

Secular Humanism is one such tare that has infiltrated the Church. What were at one time in the United States distinguished Christian Universities are now nothing but Secular Humanistic, liberal propaganda machines of ungodly reasoning and relativism. Professors, teachers, and students alike, not only in Universities but in most secondary schools as well, are proselytizing and being proselytized into Humanism and the religion of science. Mocking and demeaning anyone with Christian beliefs and values, to them, God is contrary to science and reason. Man must look to himself and to science rather than God to gain revelation and understanding. Prideful of their enlightenment and individualism, free from the "control" of family, free from all that is religious or called GOD, believing all that exist is this natural observable world therefore, there is no God, unless of course we are god! Without a God to predetermine absolute right or wrong, everyone can and must decide what is right in his or her own eyes. With no preset ethics or moral standards right and wrong can only be determined according to situation. Sounds like the book of Judges doesn't it! To their demise, Adam and Eve chose this path of independence from God.

Another tare is The Zeitgeist. And another is Liberal theology, a byproduct of the Enlightenment, which has systematically undermined the traditional view of the interpretation and authority of scripture. To liberal theologians and their followers, the Bible is not the inerrant word of God it merely in places contains the word of God. To these, scripture should be regarded as allegory emphasizing moral or spiritual lessons.

Following the doctrines of Liberal Theology and The Zeitgeist, much of the so-called "Church" or Christians today compromise with the world no longer adhering to the doctrine of sanctification and transformation. Sanctification does not mean we isolate ourselves from the world it simply means we do not conform our values, morals, and lifestyle decisions to the opinions and behaviors of the world. Much of today's Church has become little more than a

Sociopolitical and environmental organization, some of whom have gone so far as to deny the virgin birth of Christ, the very foundation of Christianity according to *Isaiah 7:14* and *Matthew 1:23*. A compromising Church, need we be reminded of the parable of the 10 virgins, without the oil for light, "the truth," sadly will miss the Wedding!

The Danger of a Fading Love

Revelation 2:3–5 (CJB)
3 You are persevering, and you have suffered for my sake without growing weary. 4 But I have this against you: you have lost the love you had at first. 5 Therefore, remember where you were before you fell, turn from this sin, and do what you used to do before. Otherwise, I will come to you and remove your menorah (lampstand) from its place — if you don't turn from your sin!

Speaking to the church in Ephesus, Jesus said, I know your works, you endured hardship and persecution and never gave up; yet He is displeased that they have grown cold in their passion and stepped back from relationship with Him. The alarming statement Jesus makes is that if they do not return to this love and close relationship He will no longer consider them His Church!

As the Church slept, the enemy came and planted tares of falsehood, deception, and apostasy, in what appears to be wheat; "the Word of truth" but is not *(Matthew 13:25)*. When Paul states in *Romans 13:11* the time is now to awaken out of sleep he uses the word *Hupnos* to exhort the Church to come out of spiritual lethargy. And if we look deeper, at its related word *Hupo "Hypo,"* from which we get the word Hypnosis, it can mean to come out from under the power, authority, and influence of someone or something. It is time for the Church that has lost its authority and power to come out from among them and once again influence and impact the world, turning it as it were, upside down *(2 Corinthians 6:17).*

Sadly, in the beginning of chapter 5 we see a resounding depiction of the current condition of much of Western Christianity, a sleeping bride. One who is unresponsive, unaware, unconscious, unable to see, hear, discern, recognize, or understand what God is doing or desires to do; uninterested in the fact He is calling them into deeper relationship. Yet fortunately we also see the Bride has not grown too cold; she still has an awareness of Him and a passion for Him; She still hears His voice and responds even at the cost of suffering ridicule and persecution. We see what many have proclaimed the Church will experience in the latter days, revival, as she is awakened, healed, and her passion aroused once again. An awakened and whole Church, one that is no longer asleep, decaying, or unresponsive, will become an unstoppable witness, one that will go into the world proclaiming and demonstrating the power of Jesus! Although persecuted for her love and commitment, she once again becomes a passionate witness full of love for Her Bridegroom. As chapter 5 closes we will see an awakening, revival, and outpouring of the Holy Spirit unlike anything since the Day of Pentecost, one that more or less began with the restoration of Israel as a nation.

How does this all begin? How is it described in the Song? It begins with an outpouring of the anointing, depicted in our story as an anointing with Myrrh; through which, the Bride is awakened and healed.

Myrrh: Awakening and Healing

Song of Solomon 5:2–5 (NKJV)
The Shulamite
2 I sleep, but my heart is awake; It is the voice of my beloved!

He knocks, saying, "Open for me, my sister, my love, My dove, my perfect one; For my head is covered with dew, My locks with the drops of the night."

3 I have taken off my robe; How can I put it on again? I have washed my feet; How can I defile them? 4 My beloved put his hand By (through) the latch of the door, and my heart yearned for him. 5 I arose to open for my beloved, And my hands dripped with myrrh, My fingers with liquid myrrh, On the handles of the lock.

I will address "My locks with drops (dew) of night" in the next chapter. The key words spoken here are myrrh, sleep, door, and lock. Myrrh means the same thing in Hebrew, Greek, Latin, and Arabic: Bitter. Scripturally it is a symbol of the suffering love of Christ. Myrrh is a gum resin acquired as gashes are cut in the bark of this small desert tree. These required cuts or gashes are reminders of the wounds (stripes) Christ received as He was beaten by the Roman soldiers.

Myrrh, a principal ingredient in the holy anointing oil, represents sanctification and was used for dedication and consecration to the Lord of both Temple articles and Priest *(Exodus 30:23–33)*. Myrrh was used for purification, cleansing, and preparation for covenant and intimacy. Purification and preparation of a Bride with myrrh *(see Esther 2:12–14)* is still practiced in some Middle Eastern Cultures. Myrrh was used in order to prepared a Bride to come before or in the presence of the King, to bring her up to the standard of royalty by cleansing and removing any unpleasant Smell (Sin being the analogy).

Myrrh speaks of sacrificial giving, an act of worship. When the Wise Men from the East came to worship the infant Jesus, they opened up their treasures giving myrrh as one of their gifts *(Matthew 2:11)*. A point I wish to make here is, treasure can suggest things kept secret, secure, or hidden.

Myrrh was used in embalming and preparation for burial *(John 19:39)*, it speaks of death, of dying to self, or in the case of Christ, dying for another! It, as said, refers to bitter that which is bitter to the taste but sweet to the smell. So myrrh in the spiritual sense speaks of the bitterness of dying to self to become a "sweet smelling aroma" to the lord. Myrrh represents suffering, sorrow, and was given to those condemned to death by crucifixion as an anesthesia in order to ease their pain and suffering. In Marks gospel we read, Jesus was given "wine mingled with myrrh" yet "He refused it."

Myrrh has been used medicinally as well as a painkiller. I read somewhere that in Chinese medicine, myrrh is used to treat the heart, liver, and spleen; these of course scripturally refer to our inner man. Myrrh is said to have direct effects on 3 specific areas of the brain: the Hypothalamus (hǐ'pō-thāl'ə-məs) which regulates the Sleep-Wake Cycle, and plays a vital role in the body's ability to maintain internal stability in response to physical shock or sudden violent disturbances which would normally prevent the ability to function normally; and the Pituitary Gland which produces a number of hormones especially those related to growth, maturity, and reproduction. And Myrrh has been used to treat the Amygdala [uh-mig-duh-luh], the control center of our emotions, a set of neurons located deep within the brain that play a key role in the emotional responses specifically those related to fear and pleasure. The Amygdala regulates passion (sex drive), social and emotional behavior, emotional balance, and the way we respond to fear, stress, anxiety, in particular triggered memories of past emotional trauma which can cause a person to respond in panic or other unhealthy ways. Abnormal function of the amygdala is said to be one cause of depression, anxiety, and phobias. Have you made the connection and recognized the spiritual and physical symbolism of myrrh to Jesus? Myrrh represents Christ's human nature, the suffering savior, and the great physician who comes to heal and restore the soul.

The Bride said: "I sleep but my heart is awake," what we see when we look deeper into this passage is again both an awaking of the Bride "Church," and a healing of her heart. Two ways we can interpret sleep, clearly she has grown cold, insensitive and indifferent to Him. As we said earlier she is a picture of the lukewarm Church whose passion has faded. She considers herself clean (righteous) and is therefore content with the religious rituals and she justifies and excuses herself for rejecting or not responding to his presence. But as was the custom in His culture, a rejected lover would anoint the doorknob of the woman he loved with myrrh as proof of his steadfast and genuine love. As Jesus said to the lukewarm church of Laodicea in *Revelation 3:20*: "behold (listen, know, understand) I am standing at the door of your heart knocking, waiting for you to open your heart to me, allowing me to enter to have a personal relationship with you. The time to respond and come out of complacency is now for far too long many in the Church have been too slow, if ever, to truly to respond to the Lord. Do not miss your time of visitation.

Also in scripture sleep also can mean to have grown old which figuratively speaks of death or dying. It speaks of one who is unhealthy, weak or faint from illness, or of a chronic condition or habit long established that is unlikely naturally to change. Nevertheless, we see His hand through the lock of the door. Door in Hebrew refers to the internal organs, the heart, the inner man, our mind, will, and emotions. He put his hand through the lock *(latch)* of the door, actually into a hole; this metaphorically speaks of a hole in her heart, her soul and emotions. There is emptiness, often a wound that He desires to touch, to fill, and to heal being spoken of here. This lock or hole for many has become, as by the Hebraic richness of meaning, a cave, a prison cell holding her heart, soul, and emotions in captivity because of bitter past traumatic experiences. Her heart, we see, was moved, aroused, awakened, healed, and came alive. This is if you have not noticed a picture of revival, the healed and revived Church. When we respond to Jesus, receiving His healing and deliverance, that which was once bitter, dead or dying becomes alive, a burning passion. Again, as she says in *Song 1:13*, He is a bundle of myrrh over her heart and in *Song 5:13* His lips (words) drip this healing as liquid myrrh.

Back to the hand, hand represents power and of course touch, again the touch of His hand to the door of her heart has left an abundance of the healing (myrrh). Notice, however, He did not open the lock or door, we must do so. Though it for a moment feel bitter or painful we must allow Jesus to touch those secret, hidden areas of pain in our soul just as He did with Peter and the woman at the well.

And then we, as with our Bride, once we respond, His touch becomes our touch, it becomes His power working through His Church!

When we respond our soul can, as David cried in *Psalm 142:7*, be brought out of prison. Delivered from the prison, the pit of distress, anxiety, sorrow, despair, and heartbreak, once bound, trapped, and controlled by circumstance or situation, or an enemy, those healed will through their praise be a witness of Jesus. In spite of persecution and wounds they may suffer, just as Peter and the woman at the well we, as this "Shulamite" bride will become an unstoppable witness going out into the world proclaiming and demonstrating the power of Jesus!

Jesus is saying today: I have come to awaken, to call out of sleep and back to the place of passion for intimacy those who have ignored or rejected my love. He is saying: let Me touch your affliction, you bitterness, and your pain. I have a healing balm in My hand, reach out and touch Me. Let the oil of joy and gladness pour out upon you and that which I deposit in you, that which I touch you with, you will deposit in and transfer to others.

Awakenings

I want to look back at a passage in the very beginning of Song of Solomon; looking deeper into what the Lord may have concealed, hidden details that after the passing of time and event we are now able to recognize. That is, His name as ointment poured forth. Or expanding the meaning, His person, character, power, and authority poured out. I believe in this statement along with verse 12 of chapter 2 Solomon was inspired to prophesy the outpouring of the Holy Spirit. Likewise chapters 3 and 5 clearly indicate awakening and revival of the slumbering Bride. Prophesied by Joel and evidenced by the events occurring on of the Day of Pentecost in Acts chapter 2, Holy Spirit was poured out upon Christ Bride as the Church began. Yet as time passed and history reveals, the Church allowed their vessels to run dry, and the power and truth began to diminish, the Spirit of the Lord began to knock on the heat of great men and women of

God, empowering them to once again set on fire His Church that she might "go about her city" bearing the praises and glory of her beloved.

The Bride states three times, *Song 2:7; 3:5; and 8:4*, each in conjunction with a reference to awakening, "I charge you, do not stir or awaken love until it pleases." Though difficult to interpret we could say it this way: Promise me, world around me, that you will not excite or bring out of sleep the love between me and my Bridegroom until He so pleases or until the time He desires for it to be awakened. It is as though Solomon prophesies that the awakenings and their timing are predetermined by Him, according to and conditioned upon His will.

What are these awakenings? First, in *Song 2:10, 13* we hear Him say, "Arise or rise up, and come away" this first awakening, again is the birth of the Church that occurred during the spring feasts of Passover and Pentecost. Her acceptance of His offer of betrothal is referred to and reiterated in *Song 2:3 and 8:5* where she was awakened under apple tree, where her mother, she who bore you, brought you forth. In chapter 3 the Bride rose up and went into streets evangelizing, bearing witness of Him and His crucifixion (palanquin) in the World. We could also speak in great detail of periods of awakening and revival through men such as Luther, Calvin, Edwards, Wesley, and Finney for example not to mention The Great Awakening(s), the Azusa Street revival, and the Charismatic Renewal. I however want to focus on the revival in chapter 5 which I believe describes the last days revival or awakening of which so many have prophesied.

Some would say revival is the slumbering, passive Church catching renewed passion, while an awakening describes nations and cultures experiencing radical change. My attempt is not a discourse on the difference between revivals and spiritual awakening rather to show Solomon seems to have prophesied such would occur. Except to point out, as history demonstrates, awakenings coincide with massive shifts and changes in society, education, science, philosophy, and technology. For example the Protestant Reformation of 1517, The Renaissance from fourteenth to the seventeenth century, the transitional period between the Middle Ages and the Modern

Ages. The Industrial Revolution mid-1700s to mid-1800s, The Age of Enlightenment, and The Age of Reason ca. 1700's where the world experienced The First Great Awakening in 1730s through men like Jonathan Edwards and George Whitefield and The Second Great Awakening 1790–1850s, Charles Finney 1820s–1830s being a prominent figure.

The postmodern era of today, post–World War II, the time of the restoration of the nation of Israel in 1948, the beginning of "the restoration of all things," in which the world has seen fundamental changes in all levels of society. In this era the Church experienced the Charismatic Renewal, again, coinciding with the restoration of Israel and Jerusalem as its capital. And in May 2018, while Post Modern Western culture undergoes radical reappraisal of culture norms, identity, history, philosophy, human nature, and morality The United States declared, before the world, Jerusalem to be the eternal capital of Israel. My question to you the reader is: do you sense in the atmosphere the urgency of the day in which we are living? It is time once again for the Church to bear witness of the power and glory of her savior, Jesus Christ.

Anointed to Bear Witness

In chapter 5 verses 4–5 we see the Bride anointed with Myrrh. Myrrh here is flowing myrrh as opposed to solid, it indicates the flowing of the Holy Spirit through her. With the anointing upon her hand and in her heart the Bride is empowered just as we see in *Luke 4:18; Acts 4:27, 10:38; and 2 Corinthians 1:21–22*. She bears witness in a hostile environment. Again, as stated in the beginning of chapter 5, it is through the Bride's description of her beloved that Solomon actually prophesies of Christ. This we will see as we perform our usual etymological mining of the Hebrew words used to describe the Bridegroom. One we will begin as soon as we leap over her first hurdle of the watchmen!

Persecution from Within: The Watchmen

The Watchmen we have discussed in much detail, even so they must once again be addressed. Of course we know there will be persecution from the world, trial and tribulation is a guarantee according to Jesus. However, I want to focus on persecution from within rather than that from the world because, as Solomon writes in *Ecclesiastes 1:9* and *3:15*, there is a cyclical nature of events experienced by Man. As it was in the beginning of the Church, in the days of the Apostles as described in the Book of Acts, so too will it be in the end of the Church Age. Major awakenings and outpourings of the Holy Spirit with signs, wonders, and demonstrations of the Glory of the Lord always seem to arouse internal condemnation. As the Bride surrenders to His touch, is awakened and revived, the watchmen are angered. Watchmen, or keepers by definition, as we said indicate those on the inside, those attempting to guard the status quo, the culture and traditions. Persecution from within arises, as they strike, wound, and attack the Bride, taking her veil in attempt to expose, shame, disgrace, and discredit this true Bride. For such is the nature of those controlled by a religious spirit, they themselves not being free hate those who are spirit and truth worshipers, as with the Pharisees, they despise those with freedom, they fear the loss of prominence and control. And, as evidenced by numerous martyrs throughout Church history, especially those during the Reformation, many "Watchmen" are willing to murder for it.

Watchmen again are mentioned twice in Song of Solomon. First in chapter 3 verses 1–4 where the Bride seeks Her Bridegroom and passes them by unharmed. So why or what would make them turn on her for evil in chapter 5? The reasons can be many, one such reason may be the "falling away" Paul speaks of for example, or they like many of the religious leaders in both Old and New Testaments are provoked by her love, commitment, and worship. The word passed by may also hold a clue. The Hebrew word used can be translated to alienate, provoke to anger, make hostile, or estrange. So she apparently has left them behind, she has realized that she is not dependent upon them in order to have relationship with this King. A fact they never wanted her to know. As with every one who is a true Bride, the true Church, relationship with Christ is never vicarious; it must be personal.

So we see a Bride whose soul becomes passionate in pursuit of her Lord is and will be persecuted. Again evidenced by the fact that they desire to take away her veil. This veil, a thin summer or outer garment worn over a dress, is her garment of praise, her worship and passion. A garment despised by religious zealots lacking passion for true worship, those who may know the Lord and believe in Him, even servants perhaps, but not friends or true disciples, those who honestly do not love the Lord. These, like the Pharisees, Sadducees, and Sanhedrin of the Bible, are those who hate passionate worshippers, who condemn them, accuse them, and attempt to discredit them, be they religious Church leaders or their ardent ideologist they bitterly slander and persecute those with a true relationship with Christ. Symbolized by the taking of her veil, we see their contempt of her, their violent attempt to stop her, and to depict her as one having no relation to Christ.

> *1 Peter 3:14–15 (NKJV)*
> *14 But even if you should suffer for righteousness' sake, you are blessed. "And do not be afraid of their threats, nor be troubled." 15 But sanctify the Lord God in your hearts, and always be ready to give a defense to everyone who asks you a reason for the hope that is in you, with meekness and fear*

Questioned: Put on Trail by the World

In verse 9 of chapter 5 she is put on trial as it were, questioned by the world, required to defend her faith. Answering their question of who, what, and why is her evangelism. She charges those who question her to accept Him as King of Kings and Lord of Lords, to become part of the Bride. She urges them to swear an oath and make a vow of covenant with this King, the same allegiance she has made by committing wholly to Him. How so? Let us look at her answer to the world and see.

As the "Body of Christ" in the dispensation of grace as we await His return and the wedding supper, it is our responsibility to feed others with the message of His Kingdom. As His life is within His Bride, she is to distribute herself to the world. As we have seen in the beginning of chapter 5 just because we have exchanged our filthy rags for His righteousness and have sanctified ourselves does not mean we can ignore the world around us. Though we suffer persecution, though coerced to compromise or remain silent we must determine to be passionate in our worship and honor of Him and to His mandate. Taking His touch, anointing, and word, one that both pierces and heals, we must demonstrate His Kingdom.

Again, I suggest to you that *Song of Solomon 5:9–16* prophetically alludes to Jesus, the Church today, and an awakening, revival, and outpouring of the Holy Spirit unlike any other since the Day of Pentecost, one that began with the restoration of the nation of Israel; one which will culminate in the very near future. This passage describes the day in which we live; a day in which a religious spirit condemns the passionate Bride; the day in which the world questions the Church, asking: "Why is your god different than all others"? Saying: "He is the same as all the rest, He is just one of many, He is just a man, why should we seek Him, why should we believe in Him, why should we obey Him"? Questions the Bride answers through a public display of worship; glorifying *"Jesus"* proclaiming and proving His Kingship, power, and glory; witnessing of His sacrificial crucifixion, the price He paid for the world.

Praise, worship, and prophetic evangelism are the expression of this revival and outpouring as the "Church," men and women, young and old alike begin to release the awakening and healing, they, as she, experienced in chapter 5 verses 4–5. When the Bride begins to evangelize, *"Anointed with myrrh"* on their hands, carrying His authority and anointing, demonstrating the Kingdom of God in the world around them, many in the world will, as did those we see In *Song of Solomon 1:4*, turn, running after Him in pursuit of His presence and glory." It is through the Bride's worship, and her declaration of praise that she answers the World's question: Who is He and why Him?

His Body

White and Ruddy

Song of Solomon 5:10 (KJV)
   The Shulamite
   0 My beloved is white and ruddy, the chiefest among ten thousand…

Echoed in the meanings of the Hebrew words Solomon uses, when she says to them: "He is White" she speaks of His purity. That He is sinless is a fact that is obvious, evident, clearly seen and understood. He is ruddy or red is the Hebrew word *"adom"* from the root word *"adam"* which is also the Hebrew word translated into English, Man, as in mankind, in *Genesis 1:26*. Both words mean red, or to show blood (in the face). In *Numbers 19:2 "adom"* describes the red heifer without spot or blemish, symbolizing pure and sinless, the burnt offering (total sacrifice) for the sin of the congregation. In *Isaiah 63* and *Revelation 19* red and blood refer to the judgment and wrath of God. So reference here is to Jesus, the second Adam, sinless, whose sacrifice and blood satisfied the wrath and judgment of God. After which, He was raised to the highest position, or as translated, exalted to the throne and right hand of the Father *[Ephesians 1:20; Philippians 2:9–10]*. She describes His exaltation to the throne of God by proclaiming Him to be the most Chief *"dagal"* meaning exalted, lifted up like a banner, conspicuous. Isaiah likewise prophesies this of Jesus:

Isaiah 11:10 (NKJV)
   10 "And in that day there shall be a Root of Jesse,
   *Who shall stand as a **banner to the people**;*
   For the Gentiles shall seek Him,
   And His resting place shall be glorious."

His Hair

Song of Solomon 5:11b (KJV)
…His locks are bushy, and black as a raven.

As She speaks of His hair things get interesting and detailed. His locks are wavy and black. The word spoken of for His hair or locks is *qevutstsoth (kev-oots-tsaw')* locks of hair or hair over forehead. It is the feminine passive participle of *quwts* or *quts (koots)* meaning in its original sense; a forelock as shorn or cut off, and interestingly refers summer either the season or summer fruit, in particular to spend the harvest season. First, we can see how this can refer to the Church Age, the time of summer between the Feast of Pentecost and Tabernacles, The period between His departure and His return. The Dispensation of Grace, the time Jesus sends those who would follow Him to reap the ready harvest.

Next, think of the word we might use "bangs" to describe the hair covering the forehead, the part hanging down. Not only did He hang on the Cross, His head dropping as He died, and breathed His last. At that moment cut off as Daniel prophesied, He was cut off but not for Himself *(Daniel 9:26)*.

Not overlooking the comment, His locks are bushy or as translated by some, wavy. The Hebrew word is *taltallim*; which figuratively refers to waving palm branches. If this foreshadow of Palm Sunday, as we refer to it were not enough, this word is from the Hebrew word transliterated *talal* which means cheated, deceived, or to mock. Which of course brings Judas and the Roman Soldiers to mind.

Last but not least, we can stretch this even further when we look three levels deep into the word black and then raven. Black here is *shachor,* which is from *shachar* meaning to turn black or grow dark as at dusk, and from a primitive root identical with *shachar* meaning to rise early or at dawn, and seek diligently. Ok, if the crucifixion, burial, and resurrection do not come to mind, well. And lest we forget, He is a rewarder and there is a tremendous reward for those who diligently seek Him *(Hebrews 11:6)*. As for the raven, two comments: one in *1*

Kings 17:6 they symbolize God's provision as they brought bread and meat to Elijah, as Jesus said of Himself in John chapter 6, His flesh is food and He is the Bread of Life. Two, in *Genesis 8* the raven suggest an emblem of God's judgment and mercy. He took upon Himself the judgment of God we deserved that we might obtain mercy.

His Lips

Song of Solomon 5:13 (KJV)
13 His cheeks are as a bed of spices, as sweet flowers: his lips like lilies, dropping sweet smelling myrrh.

The spices we have already discussed. As for His cheeks, I will only say we know His face was marred as His beard was pulled out *(Isaiah 50:6, 52:14)* in an act of abuse and shame, so here you might want to refer back to what was required to obtain and release the fragrances of the Bride.

His lips like lilies on the other hand suggest more than one might imagine. Lips *saphah* lip, speech, words, edge or boundary carries the idea of termination and, as *Strong's Exhaustive Concordance* suggest, comes from the word *caphah,* to snatch away or catch up, and is related to the word *cowph "soph"* meaning conclusion or end. Lilies: *shushan or shoshan or shoshannah,* from the tubular shape can suggest a straight trumpet. I remind you that the Bridegroom in the Jewish culture of Jesus's day would come unannounced for His bride, often at midnight, with the sound of the shofar trumpet to snatch away His bride, terminating the period of betrothal. What I am suggesting this passage points to, a point I will make in the next chapter, is indicated in the words dropping and sweet-smelling myrrh. Dropping *nataph* means to drip, and can mean to speak. Sweet smelling, *abar* ('ō-bêr), the word used here is elsewhere used to state the idea of to cross or pass over, pass through, bring or carry over. At His word, at the sound of the trumpet, His Bride will cross over, pass through, be brought somewhere, that somewhere is the home He prepared for her; I refer you to *1 Thessalonians 4:16–17.*

His Head and Fingers

Song of Solomon 5:11a, 14a (NKJV)
The Shulamite
11 His head is like the finest gold...
14 His hands are rods of gold...

"The government shall be upon His shoulder!" She speaks of His head comprised of the finest gold to speak of His kingship, one that is eternal and incorruptible. She speaks of His hand "finger," His rod of authority, and power *(Exodus 8:19; Luke 11:20)*. He is The King whose kingdom, power, and authority are eternal, without end, and as David, Isaiah, and Daniel prophesied whose body would never see corruption *(Psalm 16:10; Acts 2:27, 31; 13:34–37; Isaiah 9:6–7; Daniel 6:26)*.

Sapphire Stone: A Prophetic Rock Crying Out

Song of Solomon 14b (NKJV)
His body is carved ivory Inlaid with sapphires.

In *Luke 19:32–40* we see Jesus's response to sanctimonious religious leaders infuriated by the worship of those passionate for the Messiah.

Luke 19:37–40 (KJV)
37 And when he was come nigh, even now at the descent of the Mount of Olives, the whole multitude of the disciples began to rejoice and praise God with a loud voice for all the mighty works that they had seen; 38 Saying, Blessed be the King that cometh in the name of the Lord: peace in heaven, and glory in the highest. 39 And some of the Pharisees from among the multitude said unto him, Master, rebuke thy disciples. 40 And he answered and said

> *unto them, I tell you that, if these should hold their*
> *peace, the stones would immediately cry out.*

But what about this Stone crying out? She continues by speaking of His body made of carved Ivory, the Hebrew *shen* a word meaning teeth, sharp, pierced, a rock, figuratively meaning to imprint or scar. In other words His scared body is inlaid, overlaid, or covered, the Hebrew *alaph* also meaning to become faint or weak, after His scourging we know Jesus was weak and faint. His body (heart) is covered or inlaid with Sapphires. I might have missed this had I not read *The Audible Sapphire* in Jonathan Cahn's *The Book of Mysteries*. It is in the word sapphire that we really see the prophetic nature of this passage. Sapphire is the Hebrew word *sappir*, which is from *saphar* meaning to: tell, speak, proclaim, or show[1]. Also meaning to inscribe (carve), to number or be numbered and to score with a mark.

To score is to draw a line with a sharp instrument or to cut with incisions. It means count up debts, to keep a record, to keep account of what is required or owed of someone, in the place of another it can be a benefit accredited to. A mark indicates a sign or evidence, a visible impression for example one made by a cut or bruise, it is a symbol used to convey information, to indicate the price, or to prove ownership.

Going further *saphar* comes from *sepher* meaning a book, a scroll "register." This word can refer to a bill, a deed, a legal document indicating a right or ownership, evidence or an indictment. It can mean a letter, as we know letter in scripture refers to The Law. The Letter or Law kills, it brings the wrath or punishment of God *(2 Corinthians 3:6; Romans 4:15)*. In one sense we can see it speaks of a formal charge or accusation of a violation of the law, in another of legal evidence or documentation of a debt, a charge, a price, a purchase, and ownership. And interestingly as I studied this word *sepher* a notation said see the Hebrew word *'abedah*, meaning a lost thing. *Abedah* comes from *'abad* which refers to something lost, destruction, i.e. Hades, divine judgment, and can mean to blot out, do away with, or to destroy. *Abedah* is connected to Law, legal documents and rights, including marriage and inheritance rights, and mutual agreement between two parties.[2] I suggest one thing being spoken of here is: The Law has accused someone, someone is guilty, and someone must suffer the consequences and pay the penalty. As we now know from *Romans 10:4*, Christ is the end of the Law, He fulfilled, and paid in full, the price and punishment we deserved. Also what or whom we read of here is a reference to the kinsman redeemer who has ransomed and restored that which was lost. He has purchased our debt, paid the penalty, and accepted the punishment for the violation of God's Law and requirements of righteousness. He has restored back to us that which we lost through the First Adam. The Sapphire stone inlaid in the body of Ivory, is crying out, declaring, speaking something about the Bride and the Messiah. Initially proclaiming who He is and how He paid our debt.

Let's examine the Sapphire in more detail. The most notable and valuable sapphires are the ones we normally think of when hearing sapphire, the blue sapphire. Other varieties exist some of which are biaxial (2 axis) crystals; this of course made me think of "the Cross." These biaxial sapphires are often pleochroic *[plee-uh-kroh-ik]* displaying different shades and colors when viewed from different angles. Some appear blue when viewed at one angle, and purple from a different angle or they may be multicolored such as blue and purple.[3]

Scripturally, blue can refer to the sky or heaven. Purple represents royalty, kingship, rulership and authority *(Daniel 5:7, 16)* and is a mixture of or joining of blue and red. Red, as stated previously refers to flesh and blood; the joining of God and man, Adam (red) the color of the ground from which Adam was created. Where blue and red become or are ONE the result is Purple[4]. Jesus our king, the Word of God come down from heaven, made flesh, was clothed in a purple robe as he was accused and mocked *(John 19:2)*.

To which I will add, if you study the Tabernacle in Exodus chapters 26–27 you will notice that the gate through which man entered the outer court, the door to the Holy Place or inner Tabernacle itself, the veil before the Holy of Holies as well as the middle layer of the Tabernacle covering were all made of fine linen of blue, purple, and scarlet thread. As *John 1:14* indicates Jesus, the Word of God who dwelt, or tabernacled in Greek among us, is as He said the door, the door to salvation, the door to the Father (*John 10:7,10; Ephesians 2:10*).

Jesus's Stripes and Scars

Sapphire often contains minor inclusions of tiny slender Rutile [roo-teel] needles. These dark red minerals develop inside the sapphire crystal during formation[5].

The rutile pierces through this stone resembling the blood stained nails that pierced Jesus hands and feet, releasing us from the penalty of sin.

> *Colossians 2:14 (KJV)*
> *14 Blotting out the handwriting of ordinances that was against us, which was contrary to us, and took it out of the way, nailing it to his cross;*

Sapphire stones possessing these inclusions, when polished, can reflect or exhibit star formations referred to as asterism. Jesus is, as we know, the Bright and Morning Star *(Revelation 22:16)*!

Sapphire in Scripture

Sapphire is seen in *Lamentations 4:7* where Jeremiah speaks of the Nazirite.

> *Lamentations 4:7 (KJV)*
> *7 Her Nazarites were purer than snow, they were whiter than milk, they were more ruddy in body than rubies, their polishing was of sapphire:*

The Nazirite bodies were like polished Sapphire. Polished here is the Hebrew *gizrah*, which other than polishing can mean, a cutting or separation. It is the feminine of *gezer*, the figure or person as if cut out, cut asunder, or in pieces. In *Daniel 2:34, 44–45* we read a prophecy of a stone cut out that would destroy the kingdoms of man and establish His own everlasting Kingdom. This idea of cutting and polishing is repeatedly implied in *Song of Solomon 5* and also speaks of covenant. In *Genesis 15:17* we see covenant between God and Abraham made by the cutting in half, in pieces, the animal through which God passed as He instituted the covenant. Nazirite refers to purity and denotes one consecrated or separated to God *(Numbers 6; Judges 13; 1 Samuel 1:11)*. Nazirite speaks of one distinguished from his brothers as in Joseph in *Genesis 49:26*. Jesus of Nazareth, course the perfect Nazirite *(John 18:5, 19:19)*.

In other Scripture we read Sapphire represents Heaven, God's throne, and that which is under God's feet His authority, dominion, subjection, that which He has overcome or defeated *(Exodus 24:10; Ezekiel 1:26–28, 10:1)*.

> *Hebrews 2:8–9 (KJV)*
> *8 Thou hast put all things in subjection under his feet. For in that he put all in subjection under him, he left nothing that is not put under him. But now we see not yet all things put under him. 9 But we see Jesus, who was made a little lower than the angels for the suffering of death, crowned with glory and honour; that he by the grace of God should taste death for every man.*

The Mystery of Jesus: The Passover Lamb and the Sapphire Stone

The Lamb…had to be a male… The Passover Lamb… Every detail is significant. And in this one detail is a mystery. The word for male is the Hebrew word zachar. Zachar also means the remembrance, the recounting, the mention and the record…and to kill the zachar is to end the remembrance, to destroy the record, to wipe out the memory… And when He "Jesus" died…the remembrance of our sin also dies. The record of our guilt is destroyed. And the memory of our shame is no more… It's is also the power to end your own remembrance of your own sin and the sin of others[6].

Jesus is the destroyer of the record, the memory or a reminder of our debt and offense. The record that spoke against us, of something we owed, were guilty of, responsible for, or held accountable for, including those of someone against you. He can erase the pain and power of that which accuses you or of those things which you accuse another, anything in the past from which you cannot seem to get free. We can take all these things to another place of remembrance, the place of eradication, the Cross, even the Lord's Supper where we "remember" and activate the *releasing* work and power of Christ's crucifixion.

Jesus became flesh "man" and through His suffering and death He has identified with our pain and suffering, and yes temptations. As a result He has mercy and compassion upon us in our trials and tribulations and as *Hebrews 2:18* says gives us aid. He aids, helps, delivers, and responds to one in intense distress, supplying the needed comfort and support. And we, who have received this aid, can likewise aid others.

As said this stone means to speak. I want to make one more suggestion and that is it speaks of us, the Bride! As we know and even read in *Job 28:6*, stone is the source of sapphire. If you can hear it, we are the sapphires cut out of stone. We are both from Christ and in Christ, the chief corner stone, and the rock of offense. Upon Him, in His body, in His stripes, are our wounds, transgressions, and iniquities. When God looks at us, deep within our heart, He sees Jesus and the Cross. In Him, we along with all of our sin, suffering, pain, and sorrows, our testimonies, become something of immense beauty and value especially as we become a witness reflecting Jesus. Like the Bride in Song of Solomon, that which we have received we are able to demonstrate and release unto others with the same mercy and compassion He extended toward us, pointing them to the ONE who paid the debt of sin setting them free from its consequences. Pointing them to the ONE who gives aid, heals, and delivers. As Paul said in *2 Corinthians 4:8–10*

2 Corinthians 4:8–10 (NKJV)
8 We are hard-pressed on every side, yet not crushed; we are perplexed, but not in despair; 9 persecuted, but not forsaken; struck down, but not destroyed—10 always carrying about in the body the dying of the Lord Jesus, that the life of Jesus also may be manifested in our body.

One last thought on the Sapphire. The Sapphire in the Breastplate of the High Priest Garment, see *Exodus 30:60*, we read is in position 5. Five symbolizes Grace scripturally. The stones represented Jacob's sons. Dan was Jacob's fifth son however most scholars, and I likewise would agree that scripture does not designate him as the son the sapphire represents, but I feel the Lord showed me this. When born, Rachel said, as she named this son Dan meaning judge or judgment, saying, God has judged me. The Hebrew word here means not only a Judge, to judge, but also a defender, to defend, to vindicate. Vindicate is to clear from accusation, suspicion, to justify, to release from wrongdoing, fault, to proclaim or prove innocent. It could be said then that sapphire represents or speaks of grace in the place of judgment, and of those justified.

His Legs and His Countenance

Song of Solomon 5:15 (KJV)
15 His legs are as pillars of marble, set upon sockets of fine gold: his countenance is as Lebanon, excellent as the cedars.

Speaking of His legs and countenance, Solomon continues to prophesy of Christ and of the Brides witness. His legs described as pillars of marble suggest far more than beauty, strength, and stability. Marble, *shesh (shaysh)*, is for the most part defined as fine material, white linen, the garment or trousers worn by the High priest as he entered the Holy of Holies *(Exodus 28:42–43)*. *Shesh* is closely connected to *meshi (meh'-shee)*, meaning costly garments. Jesus, our

High priest, the mediator between God and man *(1 Timothy 2:5; Hebrews 5:10; 9:11, 24–26)*, paid the most costly price before entering the presence of God. Solomon, when he speaks of Jesus legs set upon bases of fine gold, refers beyond the price Jesus paid to that of the reward of those who accept Him. He becomes their Lord, owner, possessor, and husband *(see eden H134—base, pedestal Strong's indicates to be the same as adon H113—Sovereign, lord, master, owner. Compare also names beginning with "Adoni-")*.

His face, His appearance is as Lebanon excellent as the cedars of Lebanon. His Countenance or His human appearance is like Lebanon, again white, and her cedars speak of His majesty, power, strength, and also to purification. *(Leviticus 14:4; Numbers 19:6)*.

The word excellent, *bachar,* can be defined as acceptable, preferred, appoint, tested, or chosen, here it indicates chosen as the cedars. Remember it was from the cedars of Lebanon Solomon constructed the Temple, and Jesus of course being a tried and tested stone, the cornerstone, the sure foundation laid in Zion.

> *Isaiah 28:16 (AMP)*
> *16 Therefore the Lord God says this,*
> *"Listen carefully, I am laying in Zion a Stone,*
> *a tested Stone,*
> *A precious Cornerstone for the [secure] foundation, firmly placed.*
> *He who believes [who trusts in, relies on, and adheres to that Stone] will not be disturbed or give way [in sudden panic].*

Jesus, the stone the builders rejected was chosen by God to be the chief cornerstone *(Psalm 118:22–23)*. Not only is He the foundation, we see further detail of who He is through *bachar,* for it is the word used when God chose David to be king, to indicate Aaron's almond branch rod, once dead, resurrected, chosen by God to bud, produce life, and to indicate the one God chose to represent Him in ministry and authority.

Fine Gold

Consider once again the fine gold, we might recall the tabernacle, temple, and Ark of the Covenant were overlaid in gold, but what was it that was made of one piece of pure gold set on a base of gold? Answer, it was The Golden Lampstand, the Menorah. The candlestick in the Holy Place set before the door of the Holy of Holies where the golden Ark of the Covenant was placed and the presence of God resided.

> *Exodus 25:31, 34 (KJV)*
> *31 And thou shalt make a candlestick of pure gold: of beaten work shall the candlestick be made: his shaft, and his branches, his bowls, his knops, and his flowers, shall be of the same (of one piece).*
> *34 And in the candlesticks shall be four bowls made like unto almonds, with their knops and their flowers.*

The Menorah, placed before the entrance to the Holy of Holies, represents light, truth, the spirit of the Lord, and Christ anointed by, filled with the Spirit of God, beaten by those who crucified Him. The door we must pass through, the Truth and the Spirit that must live within us, if we are to enter the presence of God. Christ whose truth and glory we are to radiate and reflect in the world.

The Bride has in chapter 5 described His image, an image we are to be transformed into from glory to glory. But perhaps in keeping with the prophetic vein, as we close this chapter we should compare His image to that of world rulers and governments seen in Daniel.

> *Daniel 2:32–35 (KJV)*
> *32 This image's head was of fine gold, his breast and his arms of silver, his belly and his thighs of brass, 33 His legs of iron, his feet part of iron and part of clay. 34 Thou sawest till that a stone was cut out without hands, which smote the image upon his feet*

that were of iron and clay, and brake them to pieces. 35 Then was the iron, the clay, the brass, the silver, and the gold, broken to pieces together, and became like the chaff of the summer threshing floors; and the wind carried them away, that no place was found for them: and the stone that smote the image became a great mountain, and filled the whole earth.

This image in Daniel represents the kingdoms of the earth, those of man, those under the influence and control of Satan. Kingdoms growing ever more degenerate, having a measure of strength, becoming increasingly despotic, yet inglorious and divided, a Kingdom we see developing today, an attempted mixture of a multitude of nations and peoples, a kingdom Jesus, the chief cornerstone, the rock that became a great mountain, crushes as He comes with His Bride *(Revelation 19)*.

We said the world will question the Bride asking the questions: who and why of your God? In the Revival of the last days as with the time of Moses leading the Israelites out of Egypt, the Lord will show Himself strong through signs, wonders, and miracles. The Church will plunder "Egypt" if you will through a harvest of souls for the Kingdom of God. Then as in Egypt, depart.

Exodus 7:5(KJV)
5 And the Egyptians shall know that I am the Lord, when I stretch forth mine hand upon Egypt, and bring out the children of Israel from among them.

The departure of the Bride is proof to the world that God exist and that He is the God that He and the Church proclaimed Him to be.

CHAPTER 6

The Bride Taken

His first coming was to establish covenant; His second is to take His Bride home. This we will examine in chapter 6. Before doing so we need to spell out who this "perfect one" He speaks of in *Song 6:8–9* actually is. She is the wise virgin, the woman described in *Proverbs 31:29–30*, one who fears the Lord, a worshipping Bride, one obedient to His Word.

The Bride: The Bridegroom and the Wedding Chamber

According to scripture the marriage ceremony between the Bride and the Bridegroom will take place at His Father's house, as it were, under the chuppah or wedding canopy. As Heaven is a type of chuppah, we can see that when Jesus gives a shout for His bride, accompanied by the blowing of a shofar (trumpet), the marriage between Jesus and His Bride will take place in Heaven, Jesus's Fathers house.

The full marriage, the *nesu'in* in Hebrew, derived from a word meaning elevation, is completed by the chuppah. It is at this point that the Bride and groom will enter the wedding chamber, *chadar* in Hebrew, where the marriage will be consummated. At one time they would stay in that wedding chamber for seven days, or a week. At the end of the seven days, the bride and groom come out from the wedding chamber, with the Bride's veil removed she is revealed to everyone as they present themself to the world.

In chapter 6 verses 10–12, actually through verse 1 of chapter 7 in the Hebrew and other texts, we see this idea of His return and the Bride's elevation. Prophesied of in *Joel 2:5–17*, this is the moment in time when Jesus will return for His Bride. Jesus mentions this event in the *Parable of The Wedding Feast* in *Matthew 22:1–4*, the *Parable of The Wise and Foolish Virgins* in *Matthew 25:1–13*, and Paul refers to this event in *1 Thessalonians 4:16*. Because, Jesus never made random or idle comments in scripture, I suggest that you study these passages including *Matthew 7:21–23* if you have never done so. His message is clear, His heart and intent earnest, we must be qualified and prepared for the wedding, His return for His Church. An event that is sure to occur without warning, yet Jesus said, and other prophetic scriptures bear witness, the signs of the day approaching would be evident by events taking place in the Heavens, Earth, the World, and the Church, many of which have and are taking place today; the most important of which, the restoration of Israel, the Fig Tree.

As chapter 6 begins we see the Bridegroom is absent having left His Bride as His representative in her father's house. And we see the continuation of the revival from chapter 5 when suddenly His voice is heard referring to Her as an army. Solomon then begins to speak of queens, concubines, and innumerable virgins. Do we see here a world full of devout disciples of various religions or are they those Jesus spoke of in the Parable of the 10 Virgins? Keep in mind, she is proclaimed to be "the only" true Bride. Again, an army who is a reflection her King. Nevertheless, queens and concubines by definition refer to those who perhaps at one time were in covenant relationship with the King, or at least professed to such. Are they as in the Parable, which may be one of the most ominous in Scripture, the fifty percent of those invited to the wedding who are unprepared and unknown to Him, thus rejected by Him on His wedding day? Jesus makes the distinction, five are wise, having oil, and five are foolish, lacking oil. Oil is symbolic of the Holy Spirit, the Spirit of Truth, in whom the Church is sanctified, and is, as we know, the guarantee of our redemption, the guarantee of acceptance into the wedding supper of the Lamb. Something to consider, for as Paul proclaimed, preceding His return there will be a falling away, a turning away from truth, an apostasy, a divorce in no uncertain terms!

In chapter 6 there also appears to be indication of the time and season in which the wedding will take place, apparently around the time of the autumn harvest and feast, which begins with Rosh Hashanah, the Feast of Trumpets, loosely translated the "beginning," and the Feast of Tabernacles. Feast we see in verse 11 she is observing if in fact the harvest is upon her. Aware of the season, though she knows not the day nor hour He will come for her, nevertheless, she can, as Jesus said, discern the approximate soon coming hour *(Matthew 16:3; 24:32–33)*.

The Coming Bridegroom

Pertaining to the coming of the Bridegroom, I am now going to give you some Biblical information; I am going to show you some things; you do not have to agree with me, you must come to your own conclusions, but I do ask that you carefully consider what you are about to read. The Bride makes an interesting comment in *Song 6:2*, He has gone to gather His lilies. The sequence of events is crucial, before we see those stricken with awe at the disappearance of the Bride at the end of chapter 6, we see in verse 2 her beloved has gone into His garden to gather lilies. Lilies as stated in chapter2 are a metaphor for the Bride.

> *Isaiah 26:20 (AMP)*
> *Come, my people, enter your chambers*
> *And shut your doors behind you*
> *Hide for a little while until the [Lord's] [indignation, curse] wrath is past.*

In keeping with our wedding example, gathered up in His hands they are those spoken of in *Isaiah 26:20* who enter the chamber the door closing behind them. The word of significance here is "Hide." In Hebrew it is the word *chabah*, *The Brown-Driver-Briggs Hebrew and English Lexicon* indicates this to mean withdraw into privacy. *Chabah* is linked to *chabab*, love, or to hide (as in the bosom), *Brown-Driver-Briggs* says this word describes a love that is kindled or set on fire. Though previous comment has been made concerning this statement, it is again important to note that she repeatedly says throughout the Song, do not stir or awaken love until it pleases. The root of both words is *chaba*, a word used as a metaphor in *Isaiah 49:2* to describe the divine protection of Messiah. Suffice it to say, the Bride will not be subject to nor experience the wrath or as translated curse of God, for as this takes place upon the world, she will be in seclusion consummating her marriage to the King of Kings and Lord of Lords. See also *1 Thessalonians 1:10 and 5:9*, He comes to deliver us from the wrath to come.

In *Song 6:4–10* He magnifies His Bride as one who outshines all others, referring to Her as an awesome army, when suddenly, she is taken away!

> *BLOW THE SHOFAR, call a sacred assembly, gather the People—Let the Bridegroom go out from His Chamber and the Bride from her dressing room (Joel 2:15–17).*

We should recognize by now where His Chamber and her dressing room are, where He comes from and to where she departs. Of course this is heaven, His home and earth, hers. From the wedding model we see when the bridegroom returned, often at midnight, there would be a shout, "Behold, the bridegroom comes" and the sound of the ram's horn (shofar) would be blown (*Matthew 25:6; 1 Thessalonians 4:16–17; Revelation 4:1*). The Bridegroom comes with a cry and a trumpet blast, as He comes for His Bride, as she is caught up to meet Him. As *1 Thessalonians 5:2* states that day will come as a thief in the night!

1 Thessalonians 4:16–17 (KJV)
16 For the Lord himself shall descend from heaven with a shout, with the voice of the archangel, and with the trump of God: and the dead in Christ shall rise first: 17 Then we which are alive and remain shall be caught up together with them in the clouds, to meet the Lord in the air: and so shall we ever be with the Lord.

The next phase of the marriage between the bride and the groom will take place as we said under the chuppah, the wedding canopy where the marriage is to be consummated.

This is the full marriage, known in Hebrew as nesu'in. The bride and groom will go to the wedding chamber, or chadar in Hebrew, where the marriage will be consummated. They will stay in that wedding chamber for seven days, or a week. At the end of the seven days, the bride and groom will come out from the wedding chamber. This can be seen in Joel 2:16.

The word week in Hebrew is shavuah. It means a "seven." It can mean seven days or seven years. An example of the Hebrew word for week (shavuah) meaning seven years can be found in Daniel 9:24, and in 9:27, "And he [the false Messiah known as the antichrist] shall confirm the covenant with many for one week [shavuah, seven years]..." This "week" is known to Bible-believers as the tribulation period. The Jewish people understand this time to be the birthpangs of the Messiah known in Hebrew eschatology as the Chevlai shel Mashiach. This is taken from Jeremiah 30:5–7. From this we can see that the believers in the Messiah will be with the Messiah in Heaven for His wedding while the earth will be experiencing the seven-year tribulation period, or the Chevlai shel Mashiach, in Hebrew[1].

Psalm 19:4–6 A Poetic allusion of the Coming Bridegroom
The sun and its rising is likened here as the King, "Jesus" our Bridegroom coming out of His chamber. In this Psalm we see the glorifying and praising of God's Word, Jesus as we know is God's Word made or become a Man (Jn. 1:1, 14). The glory of creation is described as the

Psalm begins only to see the sun suddenly take precedence. The sun whose tabernacle is the creation of the heavens dominant yet obedient in its place and on the course God has designed for it. The sun that comes out of his place only to return there again! So it is with the servant of the Father! The Bridegroom will come out of His chamber take His Bride and return to His rightful prepared place[2].

Who is He Coming For? Those who eagerly wait and look for Him, those who hope for Him and have obeyed Him *(See 2 Peter 3:3–10; Hebrews 9:28; Revelation 22:11–17).* How do we see Her taken?

The Chariot of Her Noble People

Song of Solomon 6:12–13 (NKJV)
*   12 Before I was even aware, My soul had made me As the chariots of my noble people.*
*   13 Return, return, O Shulamite; Return, return, that we may look upon you!*
*   The Shulamite*
*   What would you see in the Shulamite As it were, the dance of the two camps?* **Mahanaim**

If you have ever read multiple translations of *Song of Solomon 6:12–13 or 7:1* in some translations you will find they often vary from translation to translation. Verse 12 of chapter 6 is considered to be the most difficult verse in the Song of Solomon to interpret. And it is easy to understand why a translator from Western culture would have difficulty when their responsibility is to maintain the context of romance and marriage. But for those who possess a basic understanding of the Ancient Jewish Wedding model and End-time prophetic scriptures the verse is not so peculiar after all.

First, we need to look back at *Song of Solomon 6:11* noticing in particular what the Shulamite Bride describes.

THE PROPHECY OF SOLOMON

Song of Solomon 6:11 (KJV)
11 I went down into the garden of nuts to see
the fruits of the valley, and to see whether the vine
flourished and the pomegranates budded.

Contrary to what some commentaries may suggest, clearly the passages that follow do not appear to be taking place at a celebration dance. No, what we see from verse 11 is she is simply taking a walk through a garden when suddenly and unexpectedly something happens to her.

Second, there are five words we need to explore from their Hebraic meaning. Soul, *nephesh*, meaning living being, the inner being of man, life, person or individual, that is the life man *"ADAM"* received as God breathed His Spirit into him; it can also mean desire, passion, appetite, and emotion. Obviously we can infer more than desire or emotion is being suggested. Chariot, *Merkabah (mer-kaw-baw')*, the feminine of *merkab (mer-kawb')*. Before we delve into all the words for chariot let it be understood, a chariot is basically a mode of transportation. Remember we read of His Chariot in Song 3:9, the Appiryon (Palanquin) which we saw was a type of Mercy Seat. Used only once in scripture we said it was the Litter, the "chariot" of the King on His day of betrothal. The Bride's Chariot in Song chapter 6 is different. This wedding carriage she speaks of is even more closely related to the Mercy Seat described in *1 Chronicles 28*.

1 Chronicles 28:18 (NKJV)
18 and refined gold by weight for the altar of
incense, and for the construction of the chariot, that
is, the gold cherubim that spread their wings and
overshadowed the ark of the covenant of the Lord.

The Hebrew word here to describe the Mercy Seat, the covering the Ark of the Covenant, is *Merkabah*. The Mercy Seat, the propitiation, in the Holy of Holies represented the Throne of God, His presence *(Exodus 25:17–22; Leviticus 16:2; 1 Samuel 4:4)*. As the High Priest approached the presence of the Lord he sprinkled the Mercy

Seat with the blood of atonement. Thus it is symbolic of Jesus, as *1 John 2:2* and *4:10* state our redemption and propitiation, who atoned for, appeased, and satisfied the demands of a Holy God *(Hebrews 9; Romans 3:25)*. The mercy seat then was the place of satisfaction whereas Jesus is the person of satisfaction. Today, we can consider The Ark of Covenant as a representation of the heart of man wherein now for the Church, is written the law of God, the heart in which God is enthroned *(2 Corinthians 3:3; Hebrews 10:16, 22)*. Now this Mercy Seat in *1 Chronicles 28:18, merkabah,* covered the Law, and as *Romans 4:14* states, The Law brings wrath, it provokes and results in punishment and indignation. We know from scripture wrath and indignation await the adversaries of God *(Isaiah 34:2; Zephaniah 3:8 Daniel 8:19+; Hebrews 10:27)*. Yet we who have accepted His mercy and redemption are not subject to such *(1 Thessalonians 1:10; 5:9)*. As Isaiah prophesied in *Isaiah 26:20*, the Bride will enter the wedding chamber, the doors will be closed; she will be hidden from God's wrath.

How might this come about? As stated the word for chariot in *Song 6:12* and *1 Chronicles 28:18* is *merkabah,* the feminine of *merkab,* a chariot, seat, or covering, both from the root Hebrew word meaning to ride, *rakab*. But what interest me the most is that this is also the root word of Chariot of fire, *Rekeb*, that took Elijah up into heaven.

> *2 Kings 2:11 (KJV)*
> *11 And it came to pass, as they still went on, and talked, that, behold, there appeared a **chariot of fire [rekeb]**, and horses of fire, and parted them both asunder; and Elijah went up by a whirlwind into heaven.*

Rekeb, the Chariot of Fire in which Elijah ascended to Heaven gets even more interesting when we realize it can mean, of a multitude, a cavalry, an "Army" Again this word as are all from *rakab*, meaning to mount "ascend upon" and cause to, or make to ride or be carried (in a Chariot). Notice the description of the Ark of the Covenant in *1 Chronicles 28*, in particular the reference to the Cherubim. Then look at Ezekiel's visions in Ezekiel chapters 1, 10, and 11 of the Cherubim. Cherubim both Ezekiel and David, in *Psalm 18*, declare God or the glory of God rode upon. Interesting! And yet, the more I read verse 12 of chapter 6 the more the word "set" or in some translations, "made me" stood out. Looking at this in the Hebrew, *sum or sim,* I noticed it could mean cause to be: seized, changed, transformed, leave, even reward. She says my soul made me as the Chariots of my noble people. Made her is important for it can be said that her soul put her, placed her or set her upon. So before she knew it, suddenly, without notice, she was seized, caught up, made to leave, and transformed.

Next we need to examine this phrase noble people, or as some translations read: Amminadib when combining *nadib,* noble and *ammi,* people. Noble here is an adjective describing her people. Her soul is the noun. Made is the verb. In Hebrew the verb is the word for the action of the noun (person, place or thing) whereas the noun, her soul, is that which is in action. So the action of her soul, that which her soul is experiencing or undergoing by the exertion of power or force is the seizing and transforming of her from one state, condition, or position to another. The symbolism is of the Chariot into God's presence by means of Mercy. The Ark of the Covenant, positioned behind the Veil inside the Holy of Holies, was approached by the High Priest through a cloud of incense and by the sprinkling of blood of Atonement. The Cherubim over the Mercy Seat represented the Throne of God, the place God's presence and voice, where He would appear in the cloud above the Mercy Seat *(Exodus 25:17–22; 1 Samuel 4:4; Leviticus 16:2)*. Like John who was told in *Revelation 4:2* to come up here "ascend" to the throne room of God in heaven, in *Song of Solomon 6:12* the Bride ascends upon the chariot or as the Holy Spirit may have encrypted in the passage, she ascends to the throne room of the Lord being as it were carried upon a chariot, carried by His mercy and atonement!

Bear with me, as I look even deeper. In Solomon's day a chariots were for Kings or nobility and in particular they were vehicles of war. So what we find in *Song 3:9* is a wedding litter, the Palanquin, something referring to that which occurred in the natural realm but in *Song 6:12* what we read of is a military vehicle and the Spiritual realm. Look further at the word noble, *nadib*, referring to princes, willing "hearted" men, a word coming from *nadab*, meaning voluntary, given as a freewill offering, volunteers, or one who has offered himself willingly, and the word people, again *ammi*, meaning nation or troops. What we find here are those riding upon the chariot are a group of people, an army of voluntary troops who have willingly given their lives to a ruler or commander. This is a very interesting passage one I think is very Prophetic especially when we look at *Genesis 32:1–2*.

> *Genesis 32:1–2 (NKJV)*
> *32 So Jacob went on his way, and the angels of God met him. 2 When Jacob saw them, he said, "This is God's camp." And he called the name of that place Mahanaim. [a] Footnotes: a. Genesis 32:2 Literally Double Camp*

After this we hear the chorus cry repeatedly, four times, *shub* translated return, come back "home" again, or answer us. Simply stated, come back so we can see you again or come back where we can see you. When the Word says something once, or when God speaks once, it is to be believed, if repeated it is to be taken seriously, how much more earnest is it when the Holy Spirit repeats something to this degree? Return repeated four times signifies a desperate cry or the cry of desperation; terror quite possibly, of those she has left behind. It shows their severe desire for her to return. You might say they were in total shock and terrified at what suddenly occurred. The Bride ask why do you want me to be in two camps, "do the dance of the of the double camp," or as the in Hebrew, the dance of the Mahanaim?

The Dance of the Mahanaim

What would you see in the Shulamite—as it were the dance of the two camps, *Mahanaim*? Dancing in Scripture and Hebrew culture was a demonstration of praise and worship, a token of joyousness "worship," especially after a victory. For example the Israelites, the Host or Armies of Israel, as God refers to them in *Exodus 12:17*, danced in celebration after the Egyptians were drowned in the Red Sea! This is what we see *in Song 6:13* when we break down the words. The Hebrew words used *Mecholah* dance and *Machaneh*, army, host, or camp of soldiers or angles. Ham·ma·ḥă·nā·yim—*the mecholat Machanayim (dance of the Machanayim)* Simply transliterated as Mahanaim, from *chanah*, an encampment of travellers or troops; figurative of dancers or angels, this is the word used in *Genesis 32* where we read of Jacob meeting the host of God's angles; Jacob called it God's camp "Mahanaim" Double camp. It was the place Jacob encounter God, where the heavens and earth connected, where the natural and spiritual realm connected.

Below the surface of the passage we see she appears to have been carried away or *"caught up"* from one company to another, from the natural world to the supernatural world, taken to celebrate her wedding in the home of her Husband! An event so traumatic to those she leaves behind they begin to cry out for her in desperation. At which time the statement "what would you see" or simply said: why are you gazing is made. A statement perhaps best understood from *Acts 1:9–11 and 1 Thessalonians 4:16–17.*

> *Acts 1:9-11 (NKJV)*
> *Jesus Ascends to Heaven*
> *9 Now when He had spoken these things, while they watched, He was taken up, and a cloud received Him out of their sight. 10 And while they looked steadfastly toward heaven as He went up, behold, two men stood by them in white apparel, 11 who also said, "Men of Galilee, why do you stand gazing up into heaven? This same Jesus, who was taken up from you into heaven, will so come in like manner as you saw Him go into heaven."*

1 Thessalonians 4:16–17 (KJV)
16 For the Lord himself shall descend from heaven with a shout, with the voice of the archangel, and with the trump of God: and the dead in Christ shall rise first: 17 Then we which are alive and remain shall be caught up together with them in the clouds, to meet the Lord in the air: and so shall we ever be with the Lord.

Who is this Shulamite Bride that is taken? As we will see she is the reflection of His glory. In *Song of Solomon 6:13 (7:1)* is actually the first time we see her name Shulamite. As a bride, scripturally the Church, she would be called by Her husband's name *(Isaiah 4:1; 65:1; 2 Chron. 7:14; Acts 15:17; James 2:7)* **O Shulamite**: more than an actual name this adjective, this title, not only signifies her as the wife of Solomon, it describes who she is or perhaps better said, has become in Him.

Song of Solomon 6:10 Complete Jewish Bible (CJB)
10 "Who is this shining forth like the dawn, fair as the moon, bright as the sun" but formidable as an army marching under banners?

Genesis 1:16–18 (KJV)
16 And God made two great lights; the greater light to rule the day, and the lesser light to rule the night: he made the stars also.
17 And God set them in the firmament of the heaven to give light upon the earth, 18 And to rule over the day and over the night, and to divide the light from the darkness: and God saw that it was good.

The moon is one of the celestial bodies created in order, by reflecting the sun, to have dominion over darkness. Consider Joseph's dream of the sun, moon, and stars bowing down to him in *Genesis*

37:9–10. Jacob identifies the symbols as himself as the sun and his wife Rachel as the moon. Scripture then has interpreted for us the sun as symbolic of a husband and the moon symbolic of a wife. *Malachi 4:2* indicates the sun symbolizes Jesus and *Psalm 19:5* likens the sun to a bridegroom. As the moon reflects the light of the sun upon or into the darkness of night, in the same manner the Bride is to reflect the light of the Bridegroom into the darkness of the world, as Paul also indicates in *1 Corinthians 11:7.* Completing the metaphor, bear in mind Paul also said in *Ephesians 2:6* we, the Bride, are seated in heavenly places in Christ.

Without a lengthy Hebrew word study here, the metaphorical question being ask is, who is this or she, *zoth an irregular feminine of zeh,* meaning lamb, who shines forth, appearing like, resembling, or having the character and appearance of *zeh,* the lamb? Likened to the Moon shining in the night, reflecting the light of the sun, so to the bride, in the darkness of this world, reflects the light of Jesus *(2 Corinthians 3:18).* And lest we forget, when those of the Church were first called Christians it was to indicate those acting like Christ. She who is like the Lamb is His reflection. As *1 John 4:17* states: As He is so are we in this World.

> *2 Corinthians 3:18 (KJV)*
> *8 But we all, with open face beholding as in a glass the glory of the Lord, are changed into the same image from glory to glory, even as by the Spirit of the Lord.*

As the Bridegroom in Song of Solomon proclaims twice, confirming the fact, she is an army. Just as *Revelation 19* clearly states the Bride is the army coming with Jesus at His second coming!

> *Colossians 3:4 (KJV)*
> *4 When Christ, who is our life, shall appear, then shall ye also appear with him in glory.*

And this army we see in *Song of Solomon 6:12*, is as prophesied in *Psalm 110:3*, an army of those who willingly offered and gave themselves to the King! The people coming with Jesus are those who had made a free will choice to follow him. As in the term Nobel People, the Bridegroom King's people shall be as volunteer soldiers, *nedabah as from nadab,* in the day He comes in His power.

> *Psalm 110 (NKJV)*
> *Announcement of the Messiah's Reign*
> *The Lord said unto my Lord, Sit thou at my right hand, until I make thine enemies thy footstool.*
>
> *2 The Lord shall send the rod of thy strength out of Zion: rule thou in the midst of thine enemies.*
>
> *3 Thy people shall be willing (volunteers)in the day of thy power, in the beauties of holiness from the womb of the morning: thou hast the dew of thy youth.*
>
> *4 The Lord hath sworn, and will not repent, Thou art a priest for ever after the order of Melchizedek.*
>
> *5 The Lord at thy right hand shall strike through kings in the day of his wrath.*
>
> *6 He shall judge among the heathen, he shall fill the places with the dead bodies; he shall wound the heads over many countries.*
>
> *7 He shall drink of the brook in the way: therefore shall he lift up the head.*
>
> *Romans 4:15*
> *15 because the law brings about wrath…*

Did you happen to notice verse 3 of *Psalm 110*? Remember in chapter 5 He states as He awakens the Bride that His locks are covered with dew! Once again, I believe Jesus is indicating to His Bride the final awakening will end in His return for His Bride. A fact confirmed when we refer to David's remark of the of the dove in *Psalm 55*. Desiring the wings of the Dove that he might fly away, fleeing from wrath, trouble, horrors, oppression, fear, and trembling, escaping the storm and tempest. In *Song of Solomon chapter 6* we see the Bride fly away in a chariot. Again, I want to stress this Chariot is symbolic of being lifted up carried away secure from the outpouring of God's Wrath, or His earthly judgment on those who in rebellion against Him have rejected Christ! The precedents are clear and repeated within Scripture. I made the comment in the beginning that God, in many ways, has in the Bible given us a Picture Book. He has more than once painted us a picture of the deliverance from His Judgment, Enoch being our first example.

Dr. Chuck Missler in "The Harpazo" writes: Enoch walked with God and God took him (Gen 5:24). We the Bride are those who walk with Christ and His Spirit (Eph. 5:8, Col. 2:6, Rev. 3:4, Gal. 5:25). Enoch wasn't "mid-flood" or "post-flood," he was "pre-flood"—removed before the flood—one person yes but we as the Church are ONE in God's Eyes one with each other, and one with Christ (John 17:11, 21–23; Galatians 3:28)[3].

Enoch was translated being taken to heaven by God *(Hebrews 11:5; Genesis 5:21–24)*. Noah, who found grace in God's eyes, just as do we "The Church," was found blameless not suffering the judgment of the unrighteous that practiced wickedness. Noah was hidden in the Ark, lifted up and spared. Righteous Lot who lived in a society openly practicing rampant perversion, a society that declared him to be intolerant and judgmental, had to be "taken out" before the judgment could come upon Sodom and Gomorrah. The pattern repeated in scripture is, no wrath until the righteous escape to safety! Careful attention should be paid to the fact that those who disbelieved and mocked this message and warning were left to face the destruction *(Genesis 19:1–29)*.

And concerning The Israelites as they departed Egypt, in the end the Egyptians so loathed the Jews they did not want them in their Land. Being desperate for them to leave, they paid them in silver and gold *(Psalm 105:37–38)*. An opinion shared by many, in particular those in the political realm and entertainment industry, those who mold and shape our Western Society.

A few final comments on this subject: Jesus said in *John 14:3* that He was going to prepare a place for His Church and would come to take her to where He is that she might be with Him. If we as the Church actually believe what we profess, that the Bible is the inspired word of God, written by men inspired by the Holy Spirit, then every "original" word written within is of significant importance whether we understand it or not. Every detail, every account, every parable, ever picture is there to convey a truth or principle. The fact that Jesus began His ministry at a wedding, that He indicated it was not His wedding, that He used symbolic language relating to the ancient Jewish Wedding, and that the Holy Spirit had men include these statements in the written Word are noteworthy. In fact, I believe if we look at scripture within the confines of the Jewish culture of the day we can avoid much of the differences of opinion, and the plethora of theological and doctrinal interpretations especially those relating to Eschatology taught today. Coloring outside the lines, if you will, we have come up with pictures and interpretations far different from the picture God intended.

As we follow the Wedding model of the ancient Hebrew culture we notice the final stage of the wedding is the Supper at the Father's house. As said, the Bridegroom would come at an unannounced moment to snatch his Bride away taking her to His home for the official wedding followed by the consummation of the covenant then the marriage feast. Perhaps alluded to in *Exodus 13:4–6* where we read of the Lord instituting a 7-day commemoration ending with a feast for the Israelites to celebrate their being taken out of Egypt. And, I believe this explains why John in the Book of Revelation mentions neither the Church nor the marriage supper after chapter 3 and until chapter 19 of Revelation. God designating the bulk of the prophecy to describe in detail Daniel's 7-year Time of Jacob's Trouble, "The Great Tribulation." The time designated for the Bridegroom and Bride to come together under the Chuppah.

So if we are as the Bible clearly states, the Bride of Christ when and how do we get to The Father's House? As stated the Bride is a purchased possession, The Church, that purchased possession, will one day *(Ephesians 4:30)* be redeemed by the power of Holy Spirit.

This is, as *Romans 8:23* speaks, the actual taking of the Bride and is the final stage of our redemption. If you cannot tolerate the word rapture, understanding of course it is simply our English translation of the Latin word *Rapturo* Jerome used to translate the Greek Harpázô in *1 Thessalonians 4:17* which means "to seize upon with force" or "to snatch up," then accept the phrase "caught up," "gathered together," or if not "snatched away" *(2 Thessalonians 2:1)*. Without attempting a detailed teaching on the difference between the Second Coming and the Rapture, the fact is we meet Him in the air not upon the earth; we will celebrate the wedding and supper, and partake together of the last Cup Jesus referred to in His Father's house. And one should always, always refer to *Colossians 3:3–4*; when Christ appears on the earth His Bride He does so with His Bride *(see also Revelation 19:11–16)* at which time Jesus, after a period of time following the Wedding Supper, returns to defeat His enemies *(Deuteronomy 20:7, 24:5)*.

CHAPTER 7
The Marriage Supper

As chapter 7 begins we see further description of the Bride. I want to focus this chapter on the actual wedding supper but feel it necessary to look at two words in particular before doing so. One is jewels in verse 1 and the other the palm tree in verse 8.

Make His Jewels

The use of the word jewels is important in that this term confirms what was said about the deliverance from the wrath awaiting those who miss the wedding. Three scripture passages alluding to this are *Isaiah 61:10, Zechariah 9:16,* and *Malachi 3:17* scriptures referring to those spared by God, and the righteous Bride clothed in salvation.

Palm

The righteous, overcoming, worshiping Bride is likened in Song of Solomon 7 to a palm tree, one that, as *Psalm 92:12* indicates, flourishes, a Bride who abundantly blooms and grows even where water "the word" is scarce. She, like the palm, is an oasis, a source of life in the dry bitter heat ridden desert. Remember, the betrothal period, the Church Age, was represented by hot summer months between Pentecost and Rosh Hashanah. She is, as the palm symbolizes in scripture, upright and righteous. She is able to withstand violent storms, the troubles she faces in life, without falling down. She is as the palm symbolizes in Ezekiel, a worshiper. The Bride is the one who has given themself to their beloved, Jesus, who in turn has taken hold of their branches. As the branches of the palm are at its head, the Bride then is one who has given their mind and will over to Christ.

The Wedding Supper of the Lamb

Above all I want you to notice in chapter 7 we see the Bride and Bridegroom together, here we read of consummation and celebration, which as we learned from the ancient Jewish Wedding Model, and *Revelation 19*, takes place at His Father's house. He now completely and totally possesses His Bride. Never again to be separated. She is royally arrayed in purple, subject to no one other than Her Bridegroom; she is now completely His. Then, as we see this moment come to an end, the couple, the Bridegroom King and His overcoming Bride, returns to her homeland.

The Marriage Supper:

> *Revelation 19:7–9 (KJV)*
> *7 Let us be glad and rejoice, and give honour to him: for the marriage of the Lamb is come, and his wife hath made herself ready.*
> *8 And to her was granted that she should be arrayed in fine linen, clean and white: for the fine linen is the righteousness of saints.*
> *9 And he saith unto me, Write, Blessed are they which are called unto the marriage supper of the Lamb. And he saith unto me, These are the true sayings of God.*

As we will see in a moment, in *Revelation 19 verse 11–21* you see the King at war, in battle! Question: What King or person goes to battle as they are celebrating a marriage or wedding? Answer: In Revelation 19 we see it is Jesus. One thing we as Believers should know is Jesus fulfills all the Law. Having said that, we must look at the law of battle in *Deuteronomy 20:7* where we read a betrothed man must remain in his home, not going into battle before married. And in *Deuteronomy 24:5* a newly married man is required to remain at home with his wife for one year.

> *Deuteronomy 20:5–7 (KJV)*
> *5 And the officers shall speak unto the people, saying, What man is there that hath built a new house, and hath not dedicated it? Let him go and return to his house, lest he die in the battle, and another man dedicate it.*
> *6 And what man is he that hath planted a vineyard, and hath not yet eaten of it? Let him also go and return unto his house, lest he die in the battle, and another man eat of it. 7 And what man is there that hath betrothed a wife, and hath not taken her? Let him go and return unto his house, lest he die in the battle, and another man take her.*

Until the house is built, the vineyard matured and the fruit thereof partaken, until marriage process is complete and the appropriate time is spent with His Bride, Jesus cannot go into battle. Clearly there is a period of time between the wedding ceremony and His return to do battle. And in case you never noticed, in Revelation chapter 19 we read that along with Jesus comes His army, and as mentioned before, that army is His Bride.

The Second Coming: The Public Appearance of the Couple

The Return to Her Home

Returning to the house of her mother, the chamber of her who conceived the Bride, the birthplace of Christianity, the place to which the Bride will return with Jesus is Jerusalem *(Song of Solomon 3:4, 8:2).*

> *Revelation 19:11–16 (KJV)*
> *Christ on a White Horse*
> *11 And I saw heaven opened, and behold a white horse; and he that sat upon him was called Faithful and True, and in righteousness he doth judge and make war. 12 His eyes were as a flame of fire, and on his head were many crowns; and he had a name written, that no man knew, but he himself. 13 And he was clothed with a vesture dipped in blood: and his name is called The Word of God*
>
> *14 And the armies which were in heaven followed him upon white horses, clothed in fine linen, white and clean. 15 And out of his mouth goeth a sharp sword, that with it he should smite the nations: and he shall rule them with a rod of iron: and he treadeth the winepress of the fierceness and wrath of Almighty God. 16 And he hath on his vesture and on his thigh a name written, **KING OF KINGS AND LORD OF LORDS.***

His army we have discussed, but if necessary you can see from the Bible; God's people are His army *(Exodus 6:26; 7:4; 12:17, 41; Numbers 33:1; Revelation 19:14).* What I would like to turn your attention to now is that she is referred to as "awesome."

Song of Solomon 6:4, 10 (KJV)
4 Thou art beautiful, O my love, as Tirzah, comely as Jerusalem, terrible as an army with banners.

10 Who is she that looketh forth as the morning, fair as the moon, clear as the sun, and terrible as an army with banners?

She is as a terrible or otherwise translated an awesome army with banners. Awesome, *ayom*, indicates terrible, dreadful, dreaded, frightful, an army with banners. Banner, *dagal*, she has been raised up, exalted, made to be conspicuous; she has also become the chief ruler along side her King. As *1 John 3:2* states, when Jesus is revealed we will be like Him. Under the banner of the Lord of Host, this conspicuous, exalted Bride who is both under and carries His Banner, returns to her home to rule and reign with her King *(2 Timothy 2:12; Revelation 5:10)*.

Servants, Friends, or Bride

Jesus said unto His disciples I no longer call you servants but friends in *John 15:15* and as in *Psalm 25:14* we find the difference between a servant and a friend is in what you know, and a Bride knows her husband intimately. Those in Covenant relationship with the Lord will be privilege to knowledge and information, blessings, and inheritance that God will not share with others. More importantly for our discussion I want you to notice that after the Wedding Jesus comes for Servants, not His friends, not the Bride!

Luke 12:36–37
*36 And ye yourselves like unto men that wait for their lord, **when he will return from the wedding;** that when he cometh and knocketh, they may open unto him immediately.*

37 ***Blessed are those servants, whom the lord when he cometh*** *shall find watching: verily I say unto you, that he shall gird himself, and make them to sit down to meat, and will come forth and serve them.*

Revelation 22:17 (KJV)
17 And the Spirit and the bride say, Come. And let him that heareth say, Come. And let him that is athirst come. And whosoever will, let him take the water of life freely.

CHAPTER 8
Her Home

As we read in *Song 2*, His first coming as the "goel," the redeemer to betroth Himself to His Bride as portrayed in the story of Ruth, was in the spring, at the time of wheat and barley harvest, the "Appointed Times" of the Feast of Passover and Pentecost. But in *Song 7:11–8:5*, we see them together returning to her place of birth at or near the fruit harvest. Note *Exodus 23:16; Deuteronomy 16:16*

> *Deuteronomy 16:16 (KJV)*
> *16 Three times in a year shall all thy males appear before the Lord thy God in the place which he shall choose; in the feast of unleavened bread, and in the feast of weeks, and in the feast of tabernacles: and they shall not appear before the Lord empty...*

> *Exodus 23:16b (KJV)*
> *And the feast of ingathering, which is in the end of the year, when thou hast gathered in thy labours out of the field*

As they arrive back to her birthplace the Bride speaks of grapes, pomegranates and fruits. She speaks of mandrakes, which symbolize among other things love, intimacy, or consummation. This group of passages seems to indicate that the consummation of all things will occur in the time of fruit harvest, the last of the "Appointed

Times" referred to as Sukkot, the Feast of Tabernacles, or the Feast of Ingathering, a feast celebrated in early autumn marking the end of or the final harvest, might we say: a final harvest of souls. The picture then is of the two advents of the Messiah, first the suffering and dying Savior at the beginning of the religious year, and second the victorious reigning King at the beginning of the secular year, Rosh Hashanah, to begin His earthly reign. The reign prophesied and one the Jews have for centuries awaited, a reign of peace on earth. In chapter 8 verse 5 when He returns the world ask: Who is this coming from the wilderness with her Bridegroom? When Jesus returns with His Bride as noted in *Revelation 19*, He sets foot on the Mt. of Olives entering Jerusalem from the east *(Zechariah 14:4–5)*, from the direction of the Dead Sea wilderness!

I Have Found "Peace" in His Eyes

Song 8:10b (NKJV)
  The Shulamite
  10 ... Then I became in his eyes as one who
found peace.

The word eye is the Hebrew *Ayin*, not only does it mean sight, it also denotes in His Presence. It can also mean in His affliction! In His eyes she found, she discovered, she obtained, and she possesses peace or favor, remember Shalom. At peace with Him she received from Him completeness, soundness, safety, and health.

When we worship, our focus, our eyes look upon Him, into His face, into His eyes; it is there we find the same. A peace they bring to her home, a time on earth as seen in chapter 8 verses 11–12 and described in *Zechariah 14:16–21* that those remaining of the earth must come yearly at the Feast of Tabernacles to pay homage to the King of Kings.

The Garden Tenant

In *Song 8:13—14* I believe we are brought back in our thoughts from the events awaiting the Church to the time in which we now live as we hear the Bridegroom speaks to the Garden Dweller: "let Me hear your voice," and we hear the Bride call out to the Bridegroom: "Make haste My Beloved." The Garden is her heart, the place the Bride hears His voice; hearing begins not in your mind, your intellect, but in your heart. Jesus in *Revelation 3:20* declares I stand at the door and knock if anyone hears… His desire is for His Bride, for intimate fellowship with her. He awaits the sound of her voice inviting Him. As John heard in *Revelation 22:17*: "The Spirit and the Bride say come"! She cries to Him to call her home as she awaits the moment He says to her: "come up here" *Revelation 4:1*.

Looking Back

The Song of Solomon has led us on the journey of the Bride becoming one with the Bridegroom, the Bride becoming "like" Him. Her development was seen in such words and statements as, "I will go to the mountain of myrrh and hill of frankincense, sapphire, the name, fragrance, and smell." As we come to verses *6–14* of chapter 8 we see from Solomon's perspective a prophetic look, and from today a reflection of this period we call the dispensation of Grace. In the end we see Song of Solomon has painted the portrait of a person, an insecure ex-slave, who progressed and matured into a King's Bride, strong in faith, unyielding, one of unquenchable faith. Many waters cannot quench her passion; nothing this world has to offer can turn her heart away. We have seen not only is the Shulamite Bride a portrait of Israel joined to God in the wilderness, she is the Church sealed with the Holy Spirit. Prophetically Solomon through the voice of the Bride cries, "Set me as a seal upon you heart and arm," a petition granted as Jesus's arms were stretched out on the cross and His hands were pierced *(Isaiah 49:16)*. Thus engraving our names in Him, in His book of life, sealing His Bride as His, assuring us that the day will come when He will redeem His purchased possession *(2 Corinthians 1:22; Ephesians 1:13—14, 4:30).*

Once more, Shulamite is not the name of the Bride rather her description, unnamed in the Song because she is in fact all of us who have entered covenant relationship with Jesus. Her story is told to remind us of who we were and where we came from. We ought to remember the word of the Lord to Peter in *Acts 10:15,* what God has called clean do not call common or unclean. Never should we accuse and condemn those who belong to Christ, but just as important we should cease condemning ourselves. We must take into account the fact that we are not common, not of the world; we are a peculiar people, a chosen, holy priesthood called to proclaim His name. Our responsibility is to labor in His vineyard, His vineyard in *Baal Hamon.* Obviously, this speaks of location, but upon closer inspection and in keeping with the theme of the Bridal army, Baal Hamon is the insignia of His rank and title, indicating He is the owner, possessor, lord and master over His unsilenced multitude, His great army. And, we His Church are His vineyard keepers, serving in and entrusted with His authority to tend and bear fruit in that vineyard.

I hope you now see and understand that Song of Solomon is more than a poem of love from God to His people Israel, and from Jesus to His Church. It is a song of the redeemed, those ready to enter the Holy of Holies. It is a song of passion, of a burning desire (fire) of the Church for Jesus and Jesus for His Church. We often talk of revival fire; herein is revival fire, that we desire intimate relationship with our Lord where nothing and no one else matters; it is the place of worship. No longer estranged we are allowed behind the veil into the Holy of Holies, the very presence of God.

Song of Solomon illustrates this deeper relationship with our Lord. Directed toward believers, it is a resounding call to return to our first love, to draw closer and more obedient to Christ, to hunger and thirst to know Jesus more. It is a prophetic unveiling of Christ and His Church. The bride behind the veil, a pure virgin, one concealed and perhaps unrecognized but soon to be revealed to the world.

She is the one John heard the voice of a great multitude speak of in *Revelation 19:7,* "the Bride who has made herself ready." A Church made ready is one who knows who she is, she knows her responsibilities as a betrothed Bride, she understands who and what she is to become.

Jesus is drawing His Church to Himself. He is waiting on our response, for us to come to Him in surrender and to receive what He desires to give to and reveal to us. The time to respond is now. And never forget the words of Christ in John 14; those who love Him, the true Bride, will keep His commandments.

In closing I refer you back to the statement of the Bride in chapter 6 verse 3; I am my beloved's *[of my beloved]* and my beloved is mine … Jewish tradition holds the acronym for this statement is Elul, the Hebraic being *aleph, lamed, vav and lamed.* Elul speaks of the end. Elul is the final month of summer the days before Rosh Hashanah the new beginning.

Sara Esther Crispe writes of this verse: *This beautiful and romantic phrase is that which represents our relationship with our Creator, which is often paralleled to that of a husband and wife, a bride and groom, in our individual lives… The month of Elul teaches us the necessity of being willing to turn around but it is not enough to have two lameds. As Rabbi Yitzchak Ginsburgh explains, in order for their to be a relationship, the two lameds need to be connected. They need to be face to face. When we turn around the second lamed to face the first, we form the image of the Jewish Heart… The Jewish heart, true love, represents a mind-to-mind, face-to-face, eye-to-eye, body-to-body, soul-to-soul connection. The vav, the connection between the head and the heart, must always stay healthy, with a clear flow. If anything cuts it off, the relationship cannot continue* [1]

The turn around the true Bride will have made. Ever keeping her eyes focused upon Her King, she guards against the little foxes that attempt to destroy their vine. She remains confident in the knowledge that in the Day of Judgment she will be free. Found to be as He is, her sins having been nullified, she has been restored to right standing with the Father.

As Jonathan Cahn has taught, *Elul 29* is *the Day of Nullification, when all debt and credit are wiped* away.[2] Cahn also says: *the month of Elul is especially important during the Shemitah,* (or as we know it the

Sabbath year). ... *During the Jubilee, the Sabbath of the land, slaves were set free, and everyone who lost their land or their ancestral possession was restored. The Jubilee was the year of restoration... The Shemitah was a blessing for Israel when they followed God, but a judgment when they did not...* [3]

The Bride is one who is no longer a slave to sin; her debt of sin has been wiped away. Based upon her decision to "marry" the King in the end she will be free from judgment. She is one who, as we have seen, has been restored, made new. Interesting, for this is the point I have sought to make from the beginning. A person is the Bride because they have a relationship with Jesus. One is a Bride of Christ when one believes He is who He said He is, has accepted the price He paid, and has their "*lamp*" filled with the oil of the Holy Spirit. The Bride is a spirit and truth worshiper, submitted under Jesus's authority, wholly devoted to Him, a sanctified reflection of Jesus as they become more and more like Him. The Bride, as the actual Hebrew reads, loves Him with her soul, with all her heart and mind, and by the decision of her will. It is a love not only effecting the emotions, it is a practical love expressed by one's lifestyle.

BIBLIOGRAPHY

Amplified Bible (AMP)
    Copyright © 2015 by The Lockman Foundation, La Habra, CA 90631. All rights reserved.

Amplified Bible, Classic Edition (AMPC)
    Copyright © 1954, 1958, 1962, 1964, 1965, 1987 by The Lockman Foundation

Complete Jewish Bible (CJB)
    Copyright © 1998 by David H. Stern. All rights reserved.

New King James Version® (NKJV®)
    Copyright Information
    The text from the New King James Version® (NKJV®) may be quoted in any form (written, visual, electronic or audio), up to and inclusive of 500 verses or less without written permission, providing the verses quoted do not amount to a complete book of the Bible, nor do verses quoted account for 25% or more of the total text of the work in which they are quoted, and the verses are not being quoted in a commentary or other biblical reference work.
    For churches requesting to use a small selection of material for church bulletins, sermons or classroom use that falls within our "gratis use" guidelines, formal written permission is not necessary. Churches may use stand-alone quotations/scriptures in sermons, bulletins, newsletters, or projected in a worship setting without asking written permission provided the translation is correctly cited.

This permission is contingent upon an appropriate copyright acknowledgment as follows:

For requests not covered by the above guidelines, write to HarperCollins Christian Publishing, Attention: Permissions Department, P.O. Box 141000, Nashville, TN 37214 or go to http://www.harpercollinschristian.com/permissions/

Introduction

1. *Dr. Chuck Missler A Message from Outside Time June 2013 Personal Update News Journal*
2. *Jewish-Hermeneutics: From Pardes (Jewish exegesis) From Wikipedia, the free encyclopedia and Rules of Jewish Hermeneutics By Rabbi Dr. Hillel ben David (Greg Killian) https://beithashoavah.org/wp-content/uploads/2014/09/Rules-of-Jewish-Hermeneutics-101.pdf*

The Ancient Jewish Wedding excerpts taken from:

Chumney, Eddie. Sources for the Jewish Wedding Ceremony. 04 02, 2008. http://thebodyofmessiah.com/fm/weddingsources.htm (accessed 07 22, 2014)

Kidner, Derek. Psalm 1–72 An Introduction & Commentary. Downers Grove, IL: Inter-Varsity Press, 1973

Lash, Neil and Jamie. Jewish Jewels. http://www.jewishjewels.org/jewish-jewels-television-series/weddings-and-marriage/(accessed 07 22, 2014)

Missler, Chuck. "Pattern is Prologue: The Rapture, Part 2: The Wedding Model." Koinoia House. 01 01, 2003. www.khouse.org (accessed 07 23, 2014)

Pragor, Reuven. "Biblical Weddings and Anniversaries." Beged Ivri. http://www.begedivri.com/wedding.htm (accessed 07 22, 2014)

Chapter 1

Kallah Strong's Exhaustive Concordance Biblehub.com
kalal Strong's Exhaustive Concordance Biblehub.com
nasa: nasah Strong's Exhaustive Concordance Biblehub.com
sakar Strong's Exhaustive Concordance Biblehub.com
Kedar Strong's Exhaustive Concordance Biblehub.com
Ruach Strong's Exhaustive Concordance Biblehub.com
Nashaq Brown-Driver-Briggs Hebrew and English Lexicon, Unabridged,
  Electronic Database. Copyright © 2002, 2003, 2006 by Biblesoft,
  Inc.
Neshiqah Strong's Exhaustive Concordance Biblehub.com

1. *Jonathan Cahn "The book of Mysteries" The Secret of Colors, p. 140*
    and The Two Waters p. 73

daka H1792 Strong's Exhaustive Concordance Biblehub.com
Shemen: H8081 Strong's Exhaustive Concordance Biblehub.com
Shem: H8034 Strong's Exhaustive Concordance Biblehub.com
Ónoma: HELPS Word-studies copyright © 1987 Biblehub.com

Chapter 2

Colossians 1:22
Unblemished: (Gr. Amomos: Unblemished), amomos (am'-o-mos)
  blameless "unblamable," without blemish "without spot," faultless
Irreproachable: above reproach (Gr. anegklétos : Irreproachable) in His
  sight—
anegklétos (an-eng'-klay-tos) a derivative of egkaleo (eng-kal-eh'-o) to
  bring a charge against; unaccused not convictable "making legal
  charges against someone in a court of law" not to be called to
  account (for sins)

1. *Lily: Singer, Isidore, PhD, Projector and Managing Editor. Entry for 'Lily'. 1901 The Jewish Encyclopedia. https://www.studylight. org/encyclopedias/tje/l/lily.html. 1901.*
2. *Lily: Fausset, Andrew R. Entry for 'Lily'. Fausset's Bible Dictionary. https://www.studylight.org/dictionaries/fbd/l/lily.html. 1949.*

Shushan, shoshan, shoshannah, Shoshannim: H7799 Strong's Exhaustive Concordance
Suws: H7797 Strong's Exhaustive Concordance

3. *Banqueting-house, Wine Brown-Driver-Briggs Hebrew and English Lexicon, Unabridged, Electronic Database. Copyright © 2002, 2003, 2006 by Biblesoft, Inc.*

Agapé: THAYER'S GREEK LEXICON, Electronic Database Copyright © 2002, 2003, 2006, 2011 by Biblesoft, Inc., biblehub.com
Agapé: HELPS Word-studies copyright © 1987, 2011 by Helps Ministries, Inc. Biblhub.com
Hinneh: H2009 Strong's Exhaustive Concordance, biblehub.com
Hen: H2005 Strong's Exhaustive Concordance, biblehub.com
Kothel H3796 Strong's Exhaustive Concordance, biblehub.com
Kedar H6938 from H6937 Qadar: Gesenius' Hebrew-Chaldee Lexicon, https://www.blueletterbible.org/study/lexica/gesenius/index.cfm)
Tselel H6738 Strong's Exhaustive Concordance, biblehub.com
Tsalal H6751 Strong's Exhaustive Concordance, biblehub.com
Bather H1334 Strong's Exhaustive Concordance, biblehub.com
Tor (tore) H8449 Strong's Exhaustive Concordance, biblehub.com
Yonah: Strong's Exhaustive Concordance, biblehub.com
Yayin: Strong's Exhaustive Concordance, biblehub.com

4. *Sensitivity of the Spirit: R. T. Kendall, Charisma Media 2002 ISBN 9780884198444... P19*
5. *Sensitivity of the Spirit: R. T. Kendall, Charisma Media 2002 ISBN 9780884198444 PP. 20–21*
6. *The Code of the Dove and the Holy Spirit Charisma Magazine charismamag.com 5/1/2013 PERRY STONE*

7. *Scripture Alphabet Of Animals: Turtle-Dove biblehub.com*

mohar H4119 Strong's Exhaustive Concordance, biblehub.com
mahar H4117 Strong's Exhaustive Concordance, biblehub.com
Adom: Strong's Exhaustive Concordance, biblehub.com
Kethem: H3800 Strong's Exhaustive Concordance, biblehub.com
Katham: H3799 Strong's Exhaustive Concordance, biblehub.com

8. *Purple: The 1901 Jewish Encyclopedia*

Eliezer H461 Eleazar, EL—God, and EZER—my helper Strong's Exhaustive Concordance, biblehub.com
Shishshim: Strong's Exhaustive Concordance, biblehub.com
Shishshim: Brown-Driver-Briggs Hebrew and English Lexicon, Unabridged, Electronic Database. Copyright © 2002, 2003, 2006 by Biblesoft, Inc., Biblehub.com
teléō G5055 and télos G5056 HELPS Word-studies Copyright © 1987, 2011 by Helps Ministries, Inc.
Kallah: Strong's Concordance Transliteration: Feminine noun Kallah or Callah: Strong's Exhaustive Concordance: bride, from the verb kalal or calah: a bride (as if perfect); perfected ("made" complete, perfect) Strong's Concordance, Strong's Exhaustive Concordance biblehub.com

9. *From Ani Lo and Dodi Li; Jonathan Cahn The Book of Mysteries p. 208, 254*

Chapter 3

Bether H1335
Rechob H7339
Rachab H7337

1. *Sanctification International Standard Bible Encyclopedia*

qumH6965
halak H1980

2. *"Leopard," Wikipedia, The Free Encyclopedia, <u>https://en.wiki-</u> <u>pedia.org/w/index.php</u>? title=Leopard&oldid=833845935 (accessed April 3, 2018).*

paralambanó G3880

Chapter 4

Chermon (kher-mone'): Hermon From charam;(khaw-ram'): Strong's Concordance, Strong's Exhaustive Concordance biblehub.com
rosh (roshe) H7218 Strong's Concordance, Strong's Exhaustive Concordance biblehub.com
Yarden H3383 Jordan, From H3381 Strong's Concordance, Strong's Exhaustive Concordance biblehub.com
abar (aw-bar') H5674 Strong's Exhaustive Concordance biblehub.com
argaman H713 Strong's Exhaustive Concordance biblehub.com
hārahṣāh H7367 or rachtsah Strong's Exhaustive Concordance biblehub.com
rachats H7366 Strong's Exhaustive Concordance biblehub.com
rachats H7364 Strong's Exhaustive Concordance biblehub.com
migdal or migdalah H4026 Strong's Concordance, Strong's Exhaustive Concordance biblehub.com
gadal H1431 Strong's Concordance, Strong's Exhaustive Concordance biblehub.com
Lebanon H3844 Lebanon From H3825 lebab H3824. lebab Strong's Exhaustive Concordance biblehub.com
shelach H7973 Strong's Exhaustive Concordance https://biblehub.com/ hebrew/7973.htm
shalach H7971 Strong's Exhaustive Concordance <u>https://biblehub.com/</u> <u>hebrew/7971.htm</u>

kopher Henna H3724 NAS Exhaustive Concordance of the Bible with Hebrew-Aramaic and Greek Dictionaries Copyright © 1981, 1998 by The Lockman Foundation All rights reserved Lockman.org
Kephir H3715, NAS Exhaustive Concordance of the Bible with Hebrew-Aramaic and Greek Dictionaries Copyright © 1981, 1998 by The Lockman Foundation All rights reserved Lockman.org
kaphar H3722

1. *Henna Fausset's Bible Dictionary Fausset, Andrew R. Entry for 'Camphire'. Fausset's Bible Dictionary. https://www.studylight.org/dictionaries/fbd/c/camphire.html. 1949.*

Nard: Morfix™, ™סקיפרומ, copyright © 2000–2018 Melingo Ltd morfix.co.il

2. *Saffron 51: Hausenblas HA; Saha D; Dubyak PJ; Anton SD (November 2013). "Saffron (Crocus sativus L.) and major depressive disorder: a meta-analysis of randomized clinical trials." Journal of Integrative Medicine 11 (6): 377–83, doi:10.3736/jintegrmed2013056 PMC 4643654 Freely accessible. PMID 24299602. 52: Lopresti AL; Drummond PD (2014). "Saffron (Crocus sativus) for depression: a systematic review of clinical studies and examination of underlying antidepressant mechanisms of action." Human Psychopharmacology: Clinical and Experimental. 29:517–27 doi:10.1002/hup.2434. PMID 25384672. From Wikipedia, the free encyclopedia*

qaneh H7070: "sweet cane" Strong's Concordance, Strong's Exhaustive Concordance biblehub.com

3. *sweet cane Fausset's Bible Dictionary*

qanah H7069 Strong's Concordance, Strong's Exhaustive Concordance biblehub.com
qinnamon H7076 Strong's Concordance, Strong's Exhaustive Concordance biblehub.com

4. *Frankincense: Easton's Bible Dictionary -Copyright Statement*

These dictionary topics are from M.G. Easton M.A., D.D., Illustrated Bible Dictionary, Third Edition, published by Thomas Nelson, 1897. Public Domain. Bibliography Information

Easton, Matthew George. Entry for 'Frankincense'. Easton's Bible Dictionary. https://www.studylight.org/dictionaries/ebd/f/frankincense.html. 1897.

lebonah H3828 Frankincense Strong's Concordance, Strong's Exhaustive Concordance biblehub.com

laban H3836: white Strong's Concordance, Strong's Exhaustive Concordance biblehub.com

Aloe: Copyright Statement

These files are public domain.

Bibliography Information

Fausset, Andrew R. Entry for 'Aloe'. Fausset's Bible Dictionary. https://www.studylight.org/dictionaries/fbd/a/aloe.html. 1949.

Spices:Copyright Statement

These files are public domain and were generously provided by the folks at WordSearch Software. Bibliography Information: Orr, James, M.A., D.D. General Editor. Entry for 'Spice; Spices'. International Standard Bible Encyclopedia. https://www.studylight.org/encyclopedias/isb/s/spice-spices.html. 1915.

Chapter 5

Hupnos G5258, Strong's Exhaustive Concordance, Biblehub.com

Hupo "Hypo" G5259, Strong's Exhaustive Concordance, Biblehub.com

adom H122 Strong's Concordance Biblehub.com

adam H119 Strong's Concordance Biblehub.com

Adam H120 Strong's Concordance Biblehub.com

dagal H1713 Strong's Concordance Biblehub.com

qevutstsoth H6977: NAS Exhaustive Concordance of the Bible with Hebrew-Aramaic and Greek Dictionaries Copyright © 1981, 1998 by The Lockman Foundation, Biblehub.com -

Brown-Driver-Briggs Brown-Driver-Briggs Hebrew and English Lexicon, Unabridged, Electronic Database. Copyright © 2002, 2003, 2006 by Biblesoft, Inc. Biblehub.com -
Strong's Exhaustive Concordance biblehub.com
quts H6972 Strong's Exhaustive Concordance biblehub.com
taltallim H8534 Strong's Exhaustive Concordance, biblehub.com: Brown-Driver-Briggs Hebrew and English Lexicon, Unabridged, Electronic Database. Copyright © 2002, 2003, 2006 by Biblesoft, Inc. biblehub.com
talal H8524 Strong's Concordance, biblehub.com: NAS Exhaustive Concordance of the Bible with Hebrew-Aramaic and Greek Dictionaries Copyright © 1981, 1998 by The Lockman Foundation, biblehub.com
shachor H7838 Strong's Exhaustive Concordance, biblehub.com
shachar H7835 Strong's Exhaustive Concordance, biblehub.com
shachar H7836 Strong's Exhaustive Concordance, biblehub.com
saphah H8193 Strong's Exhaustive Concordance, Biblehub.com
caphah H5595 Strong's Exhaustive Concordance, Biblehub.com
cowph "soph" H5490 Strong's Exhaustive Concordance, Biblehub.com
shushan H7799 Strong's Exhaustive Concordance, Biblehub.com
nataph H5197 Strong's Exhaustive Concordance, Biblehub.com
abar H5674 Strong's Exhaustive Concordance, Biblehub.com
shen H8127 Strong's Concordance Biblehub.com
alaph H5968 Strong's Concordance Biblehub.com

1. *The Audible Sapphire in Jonathan Cahn's The Book of Mysteries P. 106 FrontLine, Charisma Media/Charisma House Book Group*

sappir H5601 Strong's Concordance Biblehub.com
saphar H5608 Strong's Concordance Biblehub.com
saphar: sepher NAS Exhaustive Concordance, Biblehub.com
sepher H5612 Strong's Concordance Biblehub.com
'abedah H9 Strong's Concordance Biblehub.com
'abad H6 Strong's Concordance Biblehub.com

2. *Abedah studylight.org Bible Encyclopedias, The 1901 Jewish Encyclopedia Nov. 6 2017*

3. *+ 5. Sapphire: www.minerals.net/gemstone/sapphire_gemstone.aspx © Copyright 1997–2017 Hershel Friedman and Minerals.net, all rights reserved.*

Information on this website is the copyright of Hershel Friedman (or of others, and used with their permission). Use of any material on this website for educational purposes does not require our permission, provided it will not be published. Most of our photos are from external sources and require copyright permission from their respected copyright holders. Use of the information for any other purpose will require our explicit permission from Hershel Friedman, the copyright holder. The material on this website was created for use as a reference, for educational use, and for home use. Distribution, alteration, or usage in a commercial manner is a violation of the copyright laws and is prohibited. To obtain permission for usage, you must contact Hershel Friedman, the copyright holder.

4. From *The Purple Mystery, Jonathan Cahn The Book of Mysteries P 289, 2016 FrontLine, Charisma Media/Charisma House Book Group*

gizrah H1508 Strong's Concordance Biblehub.com
gezer H1506 Strong's Concordance Biblehub.com

5. *The Death of the Zachar p.268 The Book of Mysteries, Jonathan Cahn 2016 FrontLine, Charisma Media/Charisma House Book Group*

shesh H8336 Strong's Concordance, Strong's Exhaustive Concordance, biblehub.com
meshi H4897 Strong's Concordance, Strong's Exhaustive Concordance, biblehub.com
eden H134 Strong's Concordance, Strong's Exhaustive Concordance, biblehub.com

adon H113 *Strong's Concordance and Strong's Exhaustive Concordance, Biblehub.com*

bachar H977 *Strong's Concordance biblehub.com: NAS Exhaustive Concordance of the Bible with Hebrew-Aramaic and Greek Dictionaries Copyright © 1981, 1998 by The Lockman Foundation, biblehub.com*

Chapter 6

chabah H2247 Strong's Exhaustive Concordance Biblehub.com

chabab H2245 Strong's Exhaustive Concordance Biblehub.com

chaba H2244 Strong's Exhaustive Concordance Biblehub.com

chabah H2247 Brown-Driver-Briggs Hebrew and English Lexicon, Unabridged, Electronic Database. Copyright © 2002, 2003, 2006 by Biblesoft, Inc. Biblehub.com

chabab H2245 Brown-Driver-Briggs Hebrew and English Lexicon, Unabridged, Electronic Database. Copyright © 2002, 2003, 2006 by Biblesoft, Inc. Biblehub.com

1. *Chumney, Eddie. Sources for the Jewish Wedding Ceremony. 04 02, 2008. http://thebodyofmessiah.com/fm/weddingsources.htm (accessed 07 22, 2014)*

2. *Kidner, Derek. Psalm 1–72 An Introduction & Commentary. Downers Grove, IL: Inter-Varsity Press, 1973*

nephesh H5315 *Strong's Concordance and Strong's Exhaustive Concordance, Biblehub.com*

merkabah H4818 *Strong's Concordance and Strong's Exhaustive Concordance, Biblehub.com*

merkab H4817 *Strong's Concordance and Strong's Exhaustive Concordance, Biblehub.com*

rakab H7392 *Strong's Concordance and Strong's Exhaustive Concordance, Biblehub.com*

Rekeb H7393 *Strong's Concordance and Strong's Exhaustive Concordance, Biblehub.com sum or sim H7760 Strong's Concordance and Strong's Exhaustive Concordance*

sum or sim NAS Exhaustive Concordance of the Bible with Hebrew-Aramaic and Greek Dictionaries Copyright © 1981, 1998 by The Lockman Foundation, Biblehub.com

nadib H5081 Strong's Concordance and Strong's Exhaustive Concordance, Biblehub.com

ammi H5971 Strong's Concordance and Strong's Exhaustive Concordance, Biblehub.com

nadab H5068 Strong's Concordance and Strong's Exhaustive Concordance, Biblehub.com

shub H7725 Strong's Concordance and Strong's Exhaustive Concordance, Biblehub.com

Mahanaim H4266 Strong's Concordance and Strong's Exhaustive Concordance, Biblehub.com

Mecholah H4246 Strong's Concordance and Strong's Exhaustive Concordance, Biblehub.com

Machaneh H4264 Strong's Concordance and Strong's Exhaustive Concordance, Biblehub.com

chanah H2583 Strong's Concordance and Strong's Exhaustive Concordance, Biblehub.com

zoth H2063 Strong's Concordance and Strong's Exhaustive Concordance, Biblehub.com

zeh H2089 Strong's Concordance and Strong's Exhaustive Concordance, Biblehub.com

nedabah H5071 Strong's Concordance and Strong's Exhaustive Concordance, Biblehub.com

nadab H5068 Strong's Concordance and Strong's Exhaustive Concordance, Biblehub.com

3.   *From Dr. Chuck Missler "The Harpazo"*

Chapter 7

ayom H366 Strong's Concordance and Strong's Exhaustive Concordance, Biblehub.com

dagal H1713 Strong's Concordance and Strong's Exhaustive Concordance, Biblehub.com

Ayin H5869 Strong's Concordance and Strong's Exhaustive Concordance, Biblehub.com

Chapter 8

Baal Hamon H1174 Strong's Concordance and Strong's Exhaustive Concordance, Biblehub.com

1. *The Jewish Heart The Secret of Elul By Sara Esther Crispe, https://www.chabad.org/theJewishWoman/article_cdo/aid/424441/jewish/ The-Jewish-Heart.htm - Accessed October 23 2018*
2. *Jonathan Cahn Offers Biblical Insight on Elul 29—The Day of Nullification*

11:30AM EDT 7/9/2015 JENNIFER LECLAIRE
https://www.charismanews.com/world/50468-jonathan-cahn-offers-biblical-insight-on-elul-29-the-day-of-nullification -- Accessed October 23 2018

3. *Beyond the Shemitah with Rabbi Jonathan Cahn March 3, 2016*

http://www.daystar.com/news-updates/general-updates/beyond-the-shemitah-with-rabbi-jonathan-cahn/ -- Accessed October 23 2018

ABOUT THE AUTHOR

Mike Bates is an avid student of the Bible ever endeavoring to grow in the understanding of the Jewish roots of Christianity. He and his wife are ordained ministers currently serving in Germany. Their primary role is to instruct, equip, and encourage men and women both young and old to "do" the work of the ministry impacting the world around them through the empowerment of the Holy Spirit. Mike and his wife are members of and ordained as ministers under Pastors Ira and Linda Angustain of Kingdom Covenant Church in Lake Forest, California. Visit their website at www.mwbates.com.

CPSIA information can be obtained
at www.ICGtesting.com
Printed in the USA
FSHW021259240619
59373FS

9 781645 150831